What They're Say

In *Pursuit* of *Justice*...

* * *

"A hundred years from now Dan Hintz's book *In Pursuit of Justice* will be championed by historians as a true color representation of the life and times of a late 20th century cop. What the American conscience needs right now are more stories, books, first person accounts like this of Sheriff Hintz."

—JUSTIN ISHERWOOD
author of *Farm Kid: Tales of Growing Up in Rural America*,
journalist, *Portage County Gazette*

"This book is an engaging read and sure to draw the interest of everyone who wants to know what goes on behind the scenes in law enforcement."

—SCOTT KRUEGER
1010 WSPT-AM

"The 'police log' Dan Hintz shares is rough-edged and straightforward yet sensitive and caring. Good guys, bad guys, tragic stories, poignant moments, splashes of humor, and a new surprise in each chapter. One might hesitate to call stories about drunks, crooks, biker gangs, and right-wing extremists entertaining. But I can't figure out why."

—BILL BERRY
author, *Banning DDT:*
How Citizen Activists Led the Way

"At the height of nationwide discussion about transparency in law enforcement, Dan Hintz's book, *In Pursuit of Justice,* throws open the door and gives readers a rare, close-up look into Hintz's life and career as sheriff. The book not only recounts important history such as Hintz's takedown of the Posse Comitatus, a militant white-supremacist group, but also details the often humorous day-to-day events in law enforcement."

—SARAH MCQUEEN
Portage County Gazette

"Incredibly interesting…Dan Hintz describes the work of law enforcement over a span of decades from a perspective most citizens will never experience. Through first-hand stories and anecdotes, Hintz illuminates various facets of policing—the good, the bad, and the ugly. An amazing look into the other side of the badge."

—KATE ZDROIK
Rosholt Record

"The chapter of the Posse Comitatus will likely stand out most for general readers, a testament to the notoriety and attention the group gained in north central Wisconsin in the late 1970s through the mid- to late-1980s."

—KEITH UHLIG
Gannett Central Wisconsin Media

"Rural sheriffs don't enjoy a high profile in our law enforcement circles, yet they play a vital role in keeping the wheels of justice turning and the citizenry safe. Dan Hintz, who served as sheriff of a rural Wisconsin county for eight years, tells us just how big a role they play in this delightful book peppered with vignettes and real life experiences. In one, the former "small-town" sheriff recounts how he and his deputies defused a potentially explosive encounter with the so-called Posse Comitatus, an organization of white supremacists who believed laws didn't apply to them. This book will open eyes on just how big a part our small-town sheriffs play in all our lives."

—DAVE ZWEIFEL
editor emeritus, *The Capital Times,*
member, Wisconsin Newspaper Hall of Fame

"*In Pursuit of Justice* provides readers with insight into the stories behind the headlines of a sheriff's career in law enforcement. Having interviewed Dan Hintz for two of my radio shows, I can assure you that his stories not only make for good and enjoyable reading but they are also educational and informative."

—OLIVER K. BURROWS III
host, *Christian Economic Perspective, Hometown Morning,*
ESPN Sports Den, 1230 ESPN Radio WXCO-AM

In *PURSUIT* of *JUSTICE*

In *PURSUIT* of *JUSTICE*

Memoirs *of a* Small-Town Sheriff

DAN HINTZ
with JOHN SPILLER

FLASH *FORWARD* BOOKS

A Publishing Imprint of The Working Hour Media Group, LLC

This book is based on personal experiences, notes, and recollections.
It is a product of the author's memory and is therefore rendered as a subjective account
of events that occurred in his life. Parts of the book are based on research from
The Stevens Point Journal and *The Pointer.* Cover photo and photo on page 172
used with permission from *The Pointer.*

In *Pursuit* of *Justice*
Memoirs *of a* Small-Town Sheriff

TO MY WIFE *SHIRLEY*
AND MY THREE BEAUTIFUL CHILDREN,
DANIELLE, MICHELLE, AND KEVIN
WHOSE PATIENCE, SACRIFICES. AND UNWAVERING SUPPORT
DURING MY LAW ENFORCEMENT CAREER PROVED INDISPENSABLE
AS I PURSUED A DEMANDING YET SATISFYING PART OF MY LIFE.
FOR MY FAMILY, I WILL FOREVER BE GRATEFUL.
AND TO THE MEN AND WOMEN WHO PUT THEMSELVES IN
HARM'S WAY; THOSE WHO CHOOSE TO DEFEND THEIR COUNTRY
AND UPHOLD THE LAW. MAKING THEIR OWN SAFETY
SECONDARY IN ORDER TO PROTECT OTHERS.

THE HINTZ FAMILY, DECEMBER 1986:
SHIRLEY, DAN, DANIELLE, KEVIN, AND MICHELLE

Portage County, Wisconsin
—in the heart of the "Badger State"

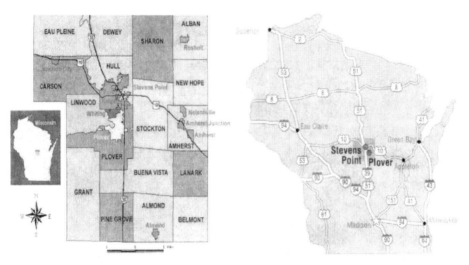

Wisconsin's nickname stems from the lead miners of the
1830s who worked in the Galena lead mines in Illinois.
These mines were located in northwestern Illinois
close to the borders of Wisconsin and Iowa.
The Wisconsin miners didn't live in houses,
but in makeshift caves called "badger dens" that
were carved into the hillsides. The miners
who lived in them were referred to as "badgers."
Through the years, the nickname stuck and
was applied to all of the people of Wisconsin
and, ultimately, to the state itself.
The badger officially became
Wisconsin's state animal in 1957.

The Village of Plover and Portage County

The Village of Plover, a quiet, rural community with scenic parks and tree-lined streets, lies in west-central Portage County. The 10.79-square-mile village—a suburb of Stevens Point—has a population of about 12,300. The 810-square-mile county—with its charming, old-time Main Streets—has a population of more than 69,000 whose demographics are mostly Polish, German, and Scandinavian.

Located between the lower and upper Wisconsin River, Plover was the first village in Portage County. In 1844, it became the county's first seat of government. In 1857, Plover was incorporated as a village, but disincorporated when Stevens Point replaced it as county seat. In 1971, Plover regained incorporation and it remains the most populated village in the county.

* * *

Portage County is bordered to the west by Wood County, to the north by Marathon County, to the east by Waupaca County, and to the south by Adams, Waushara, and Wood Counties.

Named for the portage between the Fox and Wisconsin rivers, Portage County has seventeen townships: Alban, Almond, Amherst, Belmont, Buena Vista, Carson, Dewey, Eau Pleine, Grant, Hull, Lanark, Linwood, New Hope, Pine Grove, Plover, Sharon, and Stockton. It also has nine villages: Almond, Amherst, Amherst Junction, Junction City, Nelsonville, Park Ridge, Plover, Rosholt, and Whiting.

Portage County is an outdoor lover's wonderland all year round. The county maintains thousands of acres of land and water allowing its residents to enjoy camping, fishing, hunting, and water sports. With easy access to more than forty public lakes and the Wisconsin, Plover, and Tomorrow Rivers, popular summer activities include boating, canoeing, fishing, kayaking, swimming, and waterskiing.

The county also features a first-rate system of trails, including the Green Circle Trail and Tomorrow River State Trail, which attract cyclists, hikers, and horseback riders. The 275-acre Schmeeckle Reserve, on the campus of the University of Wisconsin-Stevens Point, is a favorite among picnickers and nature enthusiasts.

Local History:
The Story of Sheriff John Baker

From 1870-1880, the Village of Plover maintained its own jail and sheriff's office. During that time, the county was under the vigilant eye of John Baker, one of the toughest sheriffs to have ever served in the county. Baker's story is an intriguing one...

The Courtright family—consisting of Amos, a farmer and father of three sons—lived in the township of Buena Vista. The Portage County Court had given Sheriff Baker an arrest warrant for Amos for failure to appear due to an unpaid mortgage lien. The sheriff, anticipating problems in arresting the notoriously ornery Amos, deputized several businessmen in Plover to form a posse. On the afternoon of October 17, 1875, they rode on horseback to the Courtright farm, which was surrounded by a white picket fence. As Sheriff Baker dismounted, Amos yelled out of a window, "Baker, if you so much as touch that gate you're a dead man!"

The sheriff had visited the farm on more than one occasion to advise the Courtrights of impending litigation against them. Amos had purportedly warned him to stay away or be shot. But Baker was a former military man who commanded a squad in the First Cavalry. Wounded in action at Shiloh, he was not only a popular man but also a brave man. On that fateful day, the sheriff passed through the gate leading to the house and was shot from a window by a rifle in the hands of Isaiah Courtwright, one of Amos's sons. Struck in the shoulder by a bullet that exited the opposite side of his stomach, Baker managed to stagger forward and return fire before his deputies rushed in and surrounded the house. While several deputies carried the sheriff to a granary on the farm, he ordering the others to torch the Courtwright house since the family refused to surrender. Sheriff Baker died twelve hours later.

In a matter of moments, the Courtwright house burned to the ground and the deputies believed that the family was consumed in the blaze. Amos Courtright and one of his sons died, but two other sons, Amos Jr. and Isaiah, escaped through a back window and then disappeared into the Buena Vista marsh where they spent the night. In the morning, they turned themselves in to the town constable in Amherst after he assured them safe transport to the county jail.

The constable chained the prisoners and placed them in a horse-drawn wagon covered with a tarp. They were safely delivered to the county jail and locked in a cell. At about 3 A.M. the next morning, a group of ten men dressed in white masks and cloaks rushed into the jail and cut off the jailer's ear. They then locked him in the cell and seized the Courtright boys. Bound and gagged, the boys were dragged behind a wagon while Sheriff Baker's pregnant wife beat them with a willow stick. They were then taken to a pine grove where they were hanged by the neck from a tree on the northwest angle of modern-day Whiting Avenue and Water Street. Both boys had been viciously beaten in the head and face before the hanging.

When news of Sheriff John Baker's death reached town, the *Plover Times* featured a story headed:

A Shocking Murder!
DEATH OF SHERIFF BAKER!
Intense Excitement!

As for Baker's funeral, the *Times* reported, "the congregation was the largest and the procession the longest we have ever witnessed in Plover."

Two small, unmarked headstones remain today in remembrance of the Courtwright brothers, buried in a common grave at Plover Cemetery in Block 2, Lot 68. As if a vast conspiracy was afoot to destroy all evidence of the crime, there is no entry of the Courtwrights in the official Register of Deaths in Portage County.

In the decades that followed a legend grew that all those who took part in the boys' hanging met violent deaths under one circumstance or another, not unlike those that befell the discoverers of King Tutankhamun's tomb.

THOSE WHO KNOW DAN BEST...

Like most any law enforcement official Dan Hintz's job entailed dealing with the media. The relationship between law enforcement and media can be contentious, but in my dealings with Dan over his four terms as sheriff, we developed a mutual trust that served us both well.

My initial dealings with Dan came when he was named the first police chief of the Village of Plover. When I had questions or sought information Dan came through for me. Reporters can't say that about all public servants they encounter.

We didn't always see eye to eye since my job was to report the news, where dealing with reporters was just one aspect of Dan's work. He had to balance the investigative process and all its ramifications with the need to provide information to the public—a test he passed with excellence.

—JAMES P. (JIM) SCHUH

former partner, vice president, columnist, Portage County Gazette;
former president and partner, WIZD-FM, Plover;
Wisconsin Broadcasters Association Hall of Fame, 2003

When I was district attorney of Portage County in the early 1970s, Dan Hintz was a young up and coming law enforcement officer. He caught my eye from the standpoint of being dedicated, hardworking, intelligent, and having the savvy to deal with difficult people and situations in a professional and evenhanded manner. So it was no surprise that Dan chose to accept the task of running the newly formed Plover Police Department in 1975. His prevailing ambition led him to leave that position to run for Portage County Sheriff in 1978 where he handily defeated the longtime incumbent.

Dan relocated to Florida in 2000 making our correspondence less frequent, but he has remained a good friend.

—MARIS RUSHEVICS

former Portage County district attorney

Dan Hintz was often referred to by the nickname "Buford" for his similarities to Sheriff Buford Pusser of McNair County, Tennessee whose story was told in the movie *Walking Tall.* Dan was a tough, no-nonsense law enforcement officer who literally carried a big stick. Although I never knew him to use his formidable piece of solid maple, it was always there just in case.

It's true that Dan was more Buford Pusser than Andy Taylor, but he did not share the former Tennessee sheriff's penchant for busting heads open. That wasn't Dan's style. He was as tough as nails, but never abusive, confident, but never cocky. Dan also had an indescribable calming effect about him. He was a great crisis manager with a knack for diffusing problems rather than making them worse.

Due to the nature of certain calls additional help was often necessary, and if the deputy's backup wasn't close, you would turn around and Dan would be there. He possessed a willingness to respond at any time of the day or night, sometimes only in shorts, a T-shirt, his badge, and his duty weapon. Dan's concern for the safety of his officers and the public was paramount.

When the Village of Plover established its police department in 1975, it named Dan Hintz as its first chief of police. He was a one-person police force until February 1976 when I became the village's first police officer. Dan and I worked together at the Plover Police Department until January 1979 when the chief was elected sheriff of Portage County and I, with help from him, took over his position. As sheriff, Dan never forgot the department he created and he assisted the Plover police whenever he could with advice, equipment, personnel and, most of all, his friendship.

With an undeniable passion for law enforcement, Dan was tough, but fair. He was compassionate, stubborn, even hardheaded at times. But he was also a determined man—one who led by example. Some people are born leaders. Dan Hintz was one of them.

Like all law enforcement officers, Dan was confronted with many dangerous situations. The way he responded to them earned him the unconditional respect of his peers. The apex of Dan's career—the removal of domestic terrorist group Posse Comitatus—gained national media coverage and warranted commendation from Wisconsin Governor Tony Earl.

Dan left behind a legacy of strength and honor in the state of Wisconsin. He was admired and respected during his nineteen-year law enforcement career; particularly, during the eight years he spent as sheriff of Portage County. He left the county law enforcement family with all flags flying, and is now "walking tall" in the world of private business. When current and retired officers and much of the public in central Wisconsin mention the name "Buford," only one person comes to mind—Dan Hintz.

—ROGER ZEBRO
retired Plover chief of police

I originally met Dan Hintz after applying for the position of patrol officer for the Plover Police Department when Dan was its chief. A physically intimidating man, Dan had the face of a bar brawler and the muscular arms and thick-barreled torso of a weightlifter. During the verbal interview, Dan began poking my chest with his steely index finger. I kept telling him to stop but he refused. The more he poked, the more he laughed. He then said to sit down and relax, that he was just checking to see what I would do when provoked.

About a week after meeting with Dan, I was called for a formal interview with local board officials. They wanted to ask me a few questions prior to their making a decision as to who would become the new patrol officer. Afterward, I ran into Dan in the hallway. He asked how I fared in the interview. "I flopped it," I told him. He said I should be proud to have made it as one of the finalists. Thinking little of it, I went home. Two hours later, my telephone rang. The man on the other end of the line asked, "Do you have any money in your wallet?"

"Who is this?" I replied.

Again, the man asked if I had any money in my wallet. "Yes, I do," I answered.

"This is Chief Hintz," the man said. "You've been selected as the new officer. I want you to go out and have a few beers to celebrate."

He then told me to be prepared to start on the following Monday morning. It was an incredible feeling to know that I would soon fulfill my dream of becoming a police officer.

On my first day riding with Dan on his rounds, we were notified of an armed robbery at a nearby minimart. "Raise your right hand," the chief said hastily, as he began swearing me in as an officer of the law right there in the squad car. He said that I would be carrying the shotgun that was kept in the car and if the suspect fired at me, I was to use the weapon in self-defense. Thankfully, no shots were fired, and the robber, a young man, was apprehended and convicted. I asked Dan if he would have shot the man had the man fired at him first. The chief told me that he never wanted to die a normal death but to die in the line of civic duty. That told me Dan was a cut above of most men and fellow police officers.

Now that I'm retired, I have a lot of time to think back on my past and one of my fondest memories is that of Dan. He was a man's man—a tough, no-nonsense kind of guy. But he was also humorous, loving, and, at times, gentle. I would have followed him into the depths of hell to complete any job we had to do. Daniel "Buford" Hintz was and will always be my friend.

—Mark J. Colrud
former Plover police officer

CONTENTS

6 Police Chief Stories

Authors' Notes

I have always wanted to work in law enforcement. Police cars with their sirens and flashing lights caught my attention as a young boy each time they drove down the streets of my hometown. Seeing local billboards of police officers leaning over to extend their hands to the children of my community made an indelible impression on me. The fact that officers could carry guns didn't hurt either. Gathering with my friends to play cops and robbers, I envisioned myself as a real police officer chasing down the bad guys, making sure they paid the price for their crimes. Law enforcement officers were my heroes and I wanted to be one of them.

It began when I stumbled across an advertisement for the Royal Canadian Mounted Police in the magazine *Outdoor Life.* I filled out the accompanying card and mailed it in. Two months later, a Royal Canadian official came to my parent's house to interview me. I was shocked that he took the time to see me, but not as shocked as he to discover that I was only fifteen years old! Still, the experience stuck with me and sustained my dream of becoming a law enforcement officer—a dream that came true in 1967 when I was hired as a sheriff's deputy in Ozaukee County. In time, I would return to my old stomping grounds in central Wisconsin to become a deputy, chief of police, and sheriff.

On the street, in a corporate office, or perhaps at a sports arena, you might find yourself surrounded by thousands of nameless people, making you believe that you are just one face in a crowd. So it's instinctive to wonder, "Why should anyone want to read about my life?" That, perhaps, is the best reason to write a memoir. As one hammers out the details of his life, and looks for what makes his journey worth reading, he also discovers what makes it worth writing. Turning the events and images of my life into a written story was more fulfilling than I had anticipated. Nevertheless, I had reservations since there is something inherently narcissistic about offering one's life story to the public.

But with the assistance of family, friends, former colleagues, and a co-author, I was able to overcome my doubts and put it all on paper. In doing so, I tried my best to ensure the accuracy of the content within this book. But even the most careful efforts can sometimes fall short of expectations. As my memory serves me, the events that follow occurred as written.

Everything in this book has been recounted "the way it happened," presented in a straightforward manner for the purpose of preserving authenticcity. I used media accounts, police reports, and mostly memories in building the book's foundation. And I did not pull punches or skirt uncomfortable truths when it came to documenting my life and career experiences. That said, not everything that happened in my life is in this book. How could it possibly be? The human memory is selective. But there is nothing in my stories that did not happen.

In Pursuit of Justice is a recollection of my childhood and adolescence, as well as experiences associated with a nineteen-year law enforcement career in central Wisconsin from the late 1960s until the first day of 1987. It depicts not only youthful discomfiture, but also family tragedies, accidents, and characters that are criminal in nature: miscreants, druggies, drunks, or just plain thugs. It also features individuals that are loveable and misguided, including those that just happened to be in the wrong place at the wrong time. During my life and particularly my law enforcement career, I came to understand that the human race isn't perfect. People make mistakes every day, but that doesn't necessarily make them bad.

After spending more than twenty-five years reciting law enforcement stories to friends and strangers alike, the response I most often encountered was, "You should sit down and write a book." So I finally did. I chose the collection of short stories within so that my readers might find at least one that stirs, reconciles, or flutters their hearts and souls in a positive, enlightening way. I hope you enjoy them.

—DAN HINTZ

Few people seem to understand what law enforcement officers endure on a daily basis. Most people will face tragedy only a few times in their lives. Officers face tragic and dangerous circumstances every day: Murder, suicide, burglaries, theft, drug trafficking, drug overdoses, sex crimes, fatal car crashes, accidental child death, and child homicide are just a few. Dealing in life or death situations puts officers on the front line in fighting crime.

Officers are also the people most likely to witness bizarre occurrences and encounter extraordinary circumstances. They see human iniquity firsthand while most citizens only catch about fifteen minutes of it on the evening news. Movies, television, and the media hardly touch upon what officers do on a daily basis.

Even so, when Dan Hintz approached me about writing his life story, I was skeptical. After all, all human beings believe they have a book in them. But when I sat down with Dan to discuss his life, I found it intriguing and worthy of recounting in print. I was also surprised to discover the level of emotion, humanity, and personal investment offered by him.

It was helpful that Dan kept scrapbooks during not only his childhood but also his law enforcement career. They consisted of photos, personal correspondence, interoffice memos, letters to the editor, and an assortment of newspaper items, all of which proved valuable in preparing the contents within.

I spent ten months interviewing Dan for this book, asking him for stories about his childhood growing up in the countryside of central Wisconsin, his service in the U.S. Army, and his nineteen-year law enforcement career. Most of those stories take place in and around Portage and Marathon Counties. What he presented in them was emotional, humorous, frightening, tragic, and, above all, revealing. It confirmed the harsh reality that crime and misfortune exist everywhere regardless of whether you live in a big city or a small county with charming towns, rustic farms, and little white churches.

Law enforcement officers have the toughest job in America—keeping the public safe in a crime-ridden society. For nineteen years, Dan Hintz was one of those officers. I hope you find his life story as enlightening as I did.

—JOHN SPILLER

All of the stories contained in this book are true. However, the names of certain persons, places, and things have been changed to protect the privacy and personal rights of individuals that are innocent, guilty, or fall somewhere in between. Such names are marked with an asterisk.

In *Pursuit* of *Justice*

Memoirs *of a* Small-Town Sheriff

A man can be as great as he wants to be.
If you believe in yourself and have the courage,
the determination, the dedication, the competitive drive,
and if you are willing to sacrifice the little things in life
and pay the price for the things that are worthwhile, it can be done.

—Vince Lombardi

PART ONE
THE FARM

Childhood Memories

*The simple hearth of the small farm
is the true center of our universe.*

—Masanobu Fukuoka

One Big, Old-Fashioned Family

Born Daniel Valentine Hintz on February 14, 1946 in Stevens Point, Wisconsin, I was the eighth of twelve children brought into the world by dairy farmers John and Bernice Hintz.

My father John, born on May 25, 1900, was the son of Polish immigrants. He passed away in December 1987. Bernice, my mother, was born on March 5, 1910 to Frank and Helen Schultz, both born and raised in America. My mother passed away in 2009, just a few months short of her one-hundredth birthday.

As for my siblings, my sister Patrinella is the Hintz family's eldest child. She is eighty-two-years young. In the eighth grade, she dropped out of school to help John and Bernice raise an ever-growing family. My brothers and sisters often referred to her as "mom" after our parents' death. Sylvester, my oldest brother, is eighty. Next in line was Lucille who passed away in 1980 at the age of forty-four. My brother Stanley died in 1989 at the age of fifty-one, and my sister Bernice was only eight years old when she passed away on December 2, 1950. My sister Delphene is seventy-two years old and my brother John, of Gurnee, Illinois, is seventy. Yours truly happens to be sixty-nine years old. My youngest brother, Jacob, was sixty-one when he died in 2007. My sister Susan was thirty-two years old when she passed away in 1980. Sixty-year-old Helen, my youngest sibling, lives in Florida. Patrinella, Sylvester, and Delphene still reside in Wisconsin.

Phyllis, the first child born to John and Bernice Hintz, died at three days old in 1929.

The Farm

My father bought a 220-acre farm in 1942 for $4,700. On its land, our family grew everything from potatoes and rutabagas to strawberries, blackberries, blueberries, tomatoes, beans, cucumbers, and carrots. My mother would can many of the vegetables along with chicken, beef, and pork ribs, so that the cellar would remain stocked for the winter.

My parents raised in upwards of 200 chickens, plus dozens of cows, ducks, geese, and hogs. In addition, fifteen or so turkeys were often turned loose in the hayfields to eat grasshoppers. Whenever my father would slaughter a hog, he would slit its throat and collect the blood for czernina, a Polish blood soup, or kiszka, a blood sausage. Although our family was hardly wealthy, we were fortunate never to go hungry—one of the benefits of living on a farm.

While growing up our family diet consisted mostly of boiled potatoes, salt pork, and homemade bread. Other than at breakfast, my mother seldom served anything else. It was mundane and redundant, but there was no such thing as a fussy eater in our family. As we sat down for supper one night in the summer of 1954, my older sister Delphene began complaining about the food on her plate. My father simply took the food away from her and told her to come back when she was hungry. A few minutes later, she returned to the kitchen table and begged to have her food back. She then devoured everything on her plate. "Eat what you're given or go hungry," my father would say. And he meant it.

While outside in the barn milking the cows in the dead of winter there was no heat source other than the animals' body warmth and an old, tattered jacket. The cattle gave off enough heat to keep themselves warm as long as the straw bedding was thick enough to keep them from coming in contact with the cold concrete. During the warmer weather in the summer, I would occasionally take naps on top of the hay inside our barn during heavy rain and thunderstorms.

Respect for farmers was something I always maintained considering that my father was one. I watched him work from sunrise to sunset on most days. Every year the man nearly broke his back planting new crops in the hope that the fickle Midwestern weather would cooperate. Sometimes it did, sometimes it didn't, but when you farm for a living, you at least have to give it try and hope for the best.

The Homestead

My parents raised their family in Shantytown—a small patch of land with two taverns and about a dozen homes clustered around a small lake within the town of Bevent in Marathon County.

One of those homes was the two-story Hintz family farmhouse. The ground level of the house consisted of a large kitchen, food pantry, living room, and two bedrooms. The second level had one large open room containing three double beds. The room had little insulation and no heat source. When the temperature plummeted in the winter, the family set up cots in the living room close to the wood-burning, smoke-belching potbelly stove to keep warm. The three feet of sawdust that insulated the stone foundation of the house helped only a little against the brutal Wisconsin winters. But the thick feather ticks made of goose down we kept on our beds helped to maintain body warmth rather nicely.

Contrary to popular belief, summers in the upper Midwest can get hot, particularly in late July through early August with temperatures rising into the upper nineties and, occasionally, the low one hundreds. With little rain or breeze the air was often stale. To cool things off a bit my father would install three-foot square fans in our windows to create airflow. He would also open the door to our basement to let in some cool, albeit musty, air.

In the absence of indoor plumbing, the Hintz house used a hand-operated pitcher pump when it was time to take a bath. A ten-gallon boiler would heat the water on our wood stove in the kitchen before we poured it into a round, two-handled metal tub. The house also had no bathrooms, only a two-seat outhouse, which seldom, if ever, had any toilet paper. Instead, we typically "cleaned up" by using pages torn out of catalogs from Sears, Alden's, or Montgomery Ward, or from thick Milwaukee-area telephone books that acquaintances would often give us. Not the most comfortable of methods, but at least it was effective.

Adolescent Obligations

Growing up on a farm meant spending many a regimented day performing seemingly endless responsibilities. For instance, a typical day during spring and early summer went something like this: Wake up at 5:30 A.M., hand milk thirty cows, put them out to pasture, and return to the house for a breakfast of fried eggs and potatoes. Then it was out to the fields to pick strawberries and haul hay until about 11:00. I ate again at about 12:30 P.M., and then it was back outside to continue hauling hay until about 4:00. After that, I returned to picking strawberries until 6:00 when it was time for a dinner of salt pork and potatoes. After eating, it was time to milk the cows again and put them out to pasture for the night. I would then return to the house for a tasty snack of strawberries sprinkled with sugar. By 10:00, it was time for a good night's sleep. Before I knew it, the sun had risen and it was time to repeat the entire routine.

As the season progressed into August and September, the harvest changed to beans and cucumbers. Still, the ritual was much the same as in the summer: Milk the cows, eat breakfast, pick three acres of beans and four acres of cucumbers (or "cukes" as my siblings and I often called them), eat an early afternoon meal, pick again, eat dinner, and milk the cows. Lunch is what my family called the snacks we often ate between meals, meaning we would eat a minimum of six to seven times per day—more fuel for the fire when working the fields.

By late September, the crop changed to potatoes. After my father's potato digger pulled the spuds from thirty acres of dirt, I picked them up by hand and threw them into burlap sacks. At the end of each day, I used a hay wagon to haul the sacks to the house where I carried them into the basement to be stored. During winters in the 1950s, my family sorted and bagged the potatoes and sold them at market for $2.50-$3.00 per 100-pound bag—a fair price at the time. Although the local children returned to school after Labor Day, the need for labor on local farms was so great that the schools would actually shut down for two weeks in early October for the harvest—a break that the kids would call "potato vacation."

During the remainder of the school year, the farm schedule lightened up a bit. Mornings started with milking the cows, then breakfast, then off to school. Since there was no bus service, I walked every day through fields and woods, a nearly two-mile trek across the central Wisconsin landscape. I loved how the sounds of morning would unfold with the dawn of country sunshine. On the most scenic mornings, the sunrise positioned a glowing layer of light atop the highest trees to the east. In the fall, birds flew overhead in the classic V-shaped flock traveling south to enjoy warmer weather. Walking through the flat, sprawling hayfields and the adjacent majestic forest, I loved gazing at the sunlight filtering through the top branches of the trees. The enchanting tunes sung by the early morning birds always put a smile on my face. The dry, crisp air, the twigs crackling under my feet as I walked on them, and the smell of the composting leaves that surrounded me, were a delight to the senses.

After arriving home from school in the winter, I would change my clothes and carry wood to the house for our potbelly stove. There was always snow to shovel at that time of the year before eating dinner and milking the cows. After returning to the house to do homework, it was time for bed.

By late May, school was out for the season. That was when the real work began. There was the spring planting which included oats, hay, beans, cucumbers, strawberries, and potatoes. There were no hay balers in our area at the time so we hauled the hay by hand and crammed it into the hayloft for winter feed for the cattle.

The Simple Life

The Hintz family appeared every Sunday at the local Catholic church with such regularity that had we ever missed so much as one mass the townsfolk probably would have come knocking on our door to make sure we were still alive.

We would attend sunrise mass at 5 A.M. and then return home, change our clothes, and milk the cows before putting them out to pasture. The rest of the day was then ours to enjoy. During the warm weather season, my brothers and I used to walk to the Plover River with our can of garden worms and fish for shiners and suckers. During cooler weather, we would take out our family's .22 caliber rifle and hunt squirrels, so long as we were home by 4 P.M. That was the time my father would make us listen to *Holy Hour* on our local AM radio station. Since we had no television, we would sit in silence around the kitchen table and listen to a one-hour sermon. My mother would prepare a big meal for the occasion, usually chicken and mashed potatoes with gravy complimented with homemade apple pies and angel food cake with strawberry sauce or molasses cookies. To my siblings and me it was the best day of the week—a much appreciated break from the standard fare of boiled potatoes, salt pork, and bread.

While growing up in Shantytown my family never had telephone service. It wasn't necessary, my father used to say. It wasn't until 1960, when I was fourteen years, old that my father finally gave in and had a phone installed in the house.

We also never had television. In fact, I never even saw a television set until I was six years old and it happened to be the one that my uncle August owned. On occasion, my siblings and I would walk two miles to his house to watch it. One particular night we tuned in to a scary Alfred Hitchcock movie called *The Squeaky Door*. When it was over, we walked home through the quiet, pitch-black countryside holding flashlights in our shaking hands, scared out of our wits.

In the 1950s, it was a big deal to attend drive-in movies. My siblings and I would rush to get our chores done to get to the theater lot by dark so we wouldn't miss the start of the movie. Failing to get our chores done on time meant no movie. My parents would take us to the drive-in about four times a year, typically on "buck nights," where as many people as possible could be stuffed into a car for the price of one dollar. At two dollars per ticket, the indoor theaters were too expensive. My mother would prepare homemade cookies and popcorn to bring with us in order to avoid paying the exorbitant prices at the concession stand. Lying on blankets, we would watch the movie on the cold hard ground. We had no way of knowing what movie was showing until we got there but it didn't matter. We were just thrilled to be at the movies!

* * *

Toward late December 1952 when I was six years old, I overheard a conversation between my father and eldest sister, Patrinella. He was reminding her how Christmas was only a couple of days away yet he had no gifts for the younger children. So my father got in his car and drove eight miles to a local sawmill on County Trunk Highway Y. He filled small onion sacks with wood chunks picked out of a scrap pile and gave each child a sack of them to be used as building blocks—a poor man's version of Lincoln Logs. He also drove to Shippy's Shoe Store in Stevens Point to buy each of his children a pair of rubber boots, the kind that fit over shoes and had a zipper on the front—first class gifts as far as the Hintz children were concerned!

As he usually did, my father would go out to the barn and butcher a few chickens or geese for our Christmas meals. Patrinella would help my mother roast the birds and make gravy to put over our boiled potatoes, quite a feast compared to what we usually ate.

Doing Without

As farmers, my parents took pride in helping to provide food for the people of central Wisconsin. But their farm was costly to operate. After the monthly bills were paid there was little, if any, money left over for the family.

As a result, I grew accustomed to wearing second hand clothes my mother would buy from rummage sales. If the clothes were too big, she would take them in or fold together any excess material with a safety pin. Some of the clothes she bought, previously worn by truckers and construction workers, were full of holes, grease, and oil stains. Other clothes had belonged to senior citizens and were at least twenty to thirty years old. The hideous appearance of my attire would prompt a great deal of teasing from my classmates at school. Making matters worse, my mom often sent me to school in mismatched shoes and battered socks. No matter how worn out they were she would patch them up and send me on my way. Because of this, two boys in my class often made fun of me. Eventually, I grew tired of the abuse and got into a fistfight with them. Even though the boys instigated the fight, I was the one that the teacher punished.

Another article of clothing the kids used to make fun of was the gaudy fur-collared woman's coat that my mother made me wear in cold weather. She trimmed the bottom between the knees and the waist to be the same length as a man's coat but it still prompted plenty of ridicule from my classmates.

The lunch pail I carried to school—a one-gallon syrup bucket, also generated plenty of schoolyard laughter. My mother pulled the stickers off the sides of the bucket, placed it in my hand, and shoved me out the door providing my classmates yet another reason to tease me.

Barefootin'

Who doesn't feel a little nostalgic remembering the childhood pleasure of walking outside barefoot? It's enjoyable to kick off one's shoes occasionally and feel the earth beneath your feet.

Other than while walking to school in the winter I never wore shoes. But walking barefoot had its hazards. Stepping on nails, broken glass, rakes, and thorns was a common occurrence for me as a child.

When I was eight years old, I jumped off a hay wagon in the barnyard and landed on a bent nail about four inches long and fully rusted. The nail penetrated my foot along the anklebone to where my father had to use vice-grip pliers to remove it. My mother had me soak my foot in Epsom salt water to clean out the wound before she bandaged it. I was then ready to go back outside and play. The thought of seeking medical help never crossed her mind. Seeing a doctor in those days required a serious injury.

Having a 1,500-pound cow step on a bare foot was nothing to laugh at either, but it happened frequently when I milked our cows by hand. As the cows stood on a cement floor, all I could do was grit my teeth and pound on the cow's foot until it lifted it. The resultant pain was an accepted part of life on a farm.

Speaking of cows, my father always stored a huge pile of manure in the barnyard through the winter since the fields were covered in snow. Come spring, I used a six-pronged fork to load the manure into wheelbarrows and then into a spreader to fertilize the soil. The color of the manure, influenced by feed, bile, and passage rate, ranged from green to black and often darkened soon after exposure to air.

Running through the fields as a young boy, I often stepped into freshly deposited, still warm piles of cow manure. As it squished between my toes, it spread a fog of obnoxious odor that irritated my nostrils for several hours. I remember my father's reaction the first time my bare feet landed in manure. "Heck, a little cow poop won't hurt ya," he said. "There's nothing to be afraid of." He was right. The feeling of soft, tepid manure between my toes is one I have never forgotten.

Too Much of a Good Thing

In the 1950s, there were no "superstores" like Walmart. So my parents used to travel eighteen miles to Stevens Point to shop at several mom-and-pop stores for the things they couldn't procure from the family farm.

My brother John and I used to look forward to when my parents went grocery shopping. We would gather our change, hop on my father's tractor, and take turns driving two miles out of town on County Trunk J to Staszak's Tavern. With its governor fully open, the tractor would rumble down the road at about thirty miles per hour. To this day, I'm surprised its engine didn't blow! For the citizens of Marathon County it wasn't a big deal to see a couple of young children driving a tractor. It was part of our way of life.

Staszak's tavern, which doubled as a store, sold fresh ice cream in five-quart buckets for ninety cents. In less than thirty minutes, my brother and I would consume an entire bucket of the frozen treat in one sitting giving us upset stomachs each time we did. But we never learned our lesson. We kept going back for more!

Lucky to be Alive

Upon returning home from school on most days, my brothers and I loved to run up the driveway to the concrete front steps of the farmhouse. However, one day in mid-December 1954 the steps were covered in ice. As it happened, I was the last in line as my brothers raced up the steps into the house. Trying to make my way behind them, I slid on the ice and fell face first onto the edge of the bottom step striking the center of my forehead, knocking me out cold; the last thing I remembered was my syrup bucket lunch pail flying out of my hand as I went down. While my brothers were shuffling about inside, my mother asked, "Where's Dan?" They told her that I was behind them when they entered the house. My mother went outside to find me lying on the cold ground bleeding from my head. She and my brothers carried me into the house, and the next thing I knew I was sitting in a chair with my head back and my mother was stuffing alcohol-soaked cotton balls into the three-inch gash in my forehead. As she tended to my injury, she began to cry; one of the few times in my life I saw her do so. Deep down she thought her son was going to die. My mother was expert at making my daily bumps and bruises feel better, but this injury surpassed all others. She cleaned it with peroxide, applied some iodine, and wrapped my head in a bandage.

Afterward, I went outside to witness a foot-wide, quarter-inch deep pool of frozen blood on the bottom step. With the severe gash on my forehead fully tended to, my mother was convinced that I was fine. So she shoved me out the door to spend the rest of the day playing outside in the cold and snow with the neighborhood kids.

Never Play with Fire

Growing up in a small town helped to give my life purpose and focus. It also taught me the consequences of making the wrong choices.

When I was nine years old, my younger brother Jacob and I decided to do something different and exciting on a rare Sunday off from chores.

After attending early morning mass, we swiped a bag of marshmallows from our mother's kitchen and headed to the nearby woods to have a roast. My father had cut a number of pine trees the previous winter for firewood, so when we came across a good-sized pine stump about one foot high we decided to build our fire on it to keep from burning the leaves that were gathered on the ground. When we lit it up, however, it took off like a torch blowing flames sky high. As my brother and I enjoyed our toasted marshmallows and laughed at each other's jokes, the flames began to flare. Before we knew it, we had started a forest fire that couldn't be controlled.

Witnessing the smoke from a watchtower, a forest ranger pulled up with a pump truck and the task of putting out the fire began. He put pumper tanks on the backs of Jacob and me and gave each of us rubber paddles with long handles to beat down the growing flames. "Stay on the edges," he yelled, "so the fire doesn't spread any further!" Soon after, a second ranger arrived in a truck pulling a chisel plow. He dredged a furrow around the fire that began to contain it. Within three hours, the two-acre blaze was extinguished.

Jacob and I were covered in soot from head to toe. "Okay boys, come over here," the ranger commanded sitting in his truck with the door open. We knew we were in trouble and were sure the ranger was going to throw us in jail. "You know you boys could've been killed out there in that fire," he said with a stern look on his face. "Yes, sir," we replied as sweat dripped from our dirty faces. He wrote our names and ages in his notebook, said "thank you," and then drove off in his truck. When Jacob and I got home, we learned that the ranger had been in contact with our parents about the fire. Consequently, my father beat our behinds with a thick twelve-inch wooden stick with split leather at the end to the point where neither of us could sit for nearly a week.

Three days later, much to our surprise, my brother and I each received a check in the mail from the Wisconsin Department of Natural Resources for $2.85 for helping fight the forest fire. Unfortunately, we had to turn the checks over to our parents.

Tragedies at Neighboring Farms

When grasshoppers, potato beetles, and walking sticks began to overwhelm farms in the upper Midwest in the 1950s, my father regularly used chemicals such as Toxaphene to combat them. But Toxaphene, a highly poisonous insecticide, would cause a number of fatalities in our region, including two in a twenty-four hour period just a mile or so from our farm.

Wearing a dust mask for protection, local potato farmer Ernie Betker was spraying his field with Toxaphene on a calm, cool day in early September 1956. His five-year-old son, Bobby,* playing outside at the time, was drawn to the sound of his father's tractor. So he decided to sprint through the potato field hoping to catch up to him. Ernie first noticed his son running behind the sprayer unit when he was half way across a forty-acre field. The farmer stopped the tractor, picked up his son, and sprinted to the farmhouse yelling to his wife to get the water running so he could flush the chemicals from the boy's bare skin. But Bobby was already showing signs of becoming ill. With his clothing saturated with the Toxaphene pesticide, he couldn't help but inhale the chemical's deadly fumes. The Betkers ran for their car and sped to Saint Michael's Hospital sixteen miles away in Stevens Point but it was too late. Their son began to convulse and was dead on arrival.

The second Toxaphene-related fatality occurred just two hours later on the same day. Ernie's cousin, Roman Wierzba, who farmed just across the Plover River, lost his six-year-old son after spraying his potato field with the deadly pesticide. The young boy was rolling a five-gallon bucket on the ground playing with it as if it were a toy. Earlier in the day, the bucket had contained pure Toxaphene. When Wierzba noticed what his son was doing, he rushed him to the house to wash him up and get him to Saint Michael's. They made it less than half way to the hospital when the boy went into convulsions. He died minutes later.

Three days after, my family attended two funerals. When the hearse pulled up to St. Ladislaw's Church in Bevent and its back door opened, the crowd witnessed two small caskets. There wasn't a dry eye to be found.

Soon after the two deaths, the Department of Natural Resources outlawed Toxaphene in the state for any use, and in 1990, the chemical left the national market.

Bill Turski* and his wife Barbara* were farmers in the Marathon County town of Hatley about five miles from our house. Acquaintances of my parents, the Turskis attended the same Catholic church as us. On July 25, 1952, Bill suffered an accident involving a flatbed chopper used for cutting corn into short chunks to produce silage.

While using the machine to propel the corn silage up into his silo, Bill noticed that an ear of corn had become wedged under its wheel. When he tried to remove it, his arm became stuck causing the machine to pull in his entire body. Barbara, who was washing dishes in the house at the time, thought it suspicious that the machine was making a whining noise instead of its usual chopping sound. So she stopped what she was doing and went outside to see what was happening. She yelled for her husband but he was nowhere to be found. She then climbed up the external steps of the silo to have a peek inside. Looking down Barbara saw a circle of red in the middle of the corn silage, but had no idea what it was. When she got a little closer, however, she witnessed a shocking scene: Lying on top of the silage was a neatly formed pyramid of blood, bones, and flesh that used to be her husband. The corn-chopping machine had minced the farmer's body like ground hamburger.

* * *

A different accident that occurred near our farm involved Ludwig Flees, a twenty-five-year-old truck driver and family friend. On September 3, 1957, our next-door neighbor Leo Wierzba, also a farmer, happened to be working on his tractor when he witnessed the accident.

After traveling down County Trunk J, Ludwig's truck veered off the road into a gentle ditch at the edge of our neighbor's driveway. The truck, loaded to the brim with gasoline, stood on its nose and made a 360 degree spin. The truck's driver's-side door swung open allowing the young man to jump out. As he did, however, the truck fell directly on top of him forcing his body into the ground. My father and Leo came to Ludwig's aid with hydraulic tractors and the two farmers worked diligently to lift the truck off the man, but to no avail. They grabbed their shovels and tried digging Ludwig out manually but the weight of the truck on his body proved too much to overcome. Watching nearby, all I could see of the driver were the ends of his hands and feet protruding from under the truck.

As my father kept digging, Leo informed the sheriff's department of the accident, and less than an hour later, a huge wrecking vehicle from Wausau Homes arrived at the scene. Although the truck was lifted, Ludwig had died on impact under its tremendous weight, his crushed body driven well into the dirt of the hay field.

A sheriff's department investigation at the accident scene found that a tie rod had fallen off the gasoline truck. Landing in Ludwig's path, the rod caused the truck to veer off the road. Though the young man wasn't traveling at a high rate of speed, it was still enough to where the truck was able to make a complete standing revolution. Fortunately, the gallons of fuel pouring out of the vehicle didn't ignite—something my father and Leo considered a miracle.

Ludwig's parents held a humble wake for their son, who was single and didn't have a family of his own, in the living room of their home.

Alan Adamczyk,* a farmer and construction worker who lived roughly four miles from our farm, was known to struggle with depression. A good friend of my parents, I remember him as high strung, nervous, and easily upset. The fact that Alan's wife preferred to do all the talking and set all the rules in the Adamczyk household purportedly troubled him.

In the summer of 1959, Alan attempted to commit suicide on a number of occasions. In one case, he unscrewed the glass fuses from a fuse box in his home and plugged his fingers into the sockets to try to electrocute himself. Though it burned the heck out of his hands, the currents weren't strong enough to kill him.

Alan disappeared one day in late August of that year. When his family went looking for him, they found his limp body hanging from the limb of a nearby tree with baler twine wrapped around the neck. He had finally succeeded in taking his life.

Family Illness

In early 1949 when I was nearly three years old, my mother Bernice was diagnosed with tuberculosis. The potentially fatal disease caused her to be quarantined in the River Pines Sanatorium in Stevens Point. My fourteen-year-old sister Patrinella, in eighth grade at the time, dropped out of school to help my father raise the family. Things were tough without my mother around but Patrinella was the next closest thing for my siblings and me.

My mother's absence was particularly tough on my father. A strong, but internally emotional man, he would go to his bedroom after Sunday morning church service, lock the door behind him, and cry his eyes out. Missing his wife—the woman he loved more than anything in the world—it was heartbreaking to see my father this way.

After three long and exasperating years, my mother came home from the sanatorium and our lives resumed normalcy.

"Junie"

Death leaves a heartache no one can heal,
love leaves a memory no one can steal.
—Richard Puz, *The Carolinian*

My life as a child wasn't without tragedy. When I was four years old one of my elder sisters, Bernice—who we called "Junie," as in "Junior," since she had the same name as my mother—suddenly became ill. At the age of eight, Junie, a beautiful, friendly young girl, shared in the responsibility of taking care of her younger siblings especially while the older siblings were working in the field with my father.

At around 2 A.M. on November 27, 1950, a blood-curdling scream woke me out of a sound sleep. I saw that the light was on in Junie's bedroom so I went to see what was going on. Patrinella was standing next to Junie's bed calling for my father to come quick, that something was terribly wrong. Junie was lying on the bed in a fetal position holding her stomach in excruciating pain. With my mother in the sanatorium, my father and Patrinella hurriedly dressed her, carried her to the family car, and then rushed her to Saint Michael's. While performing emergency surgery on Junie, Dr. Miller, the family physician, discovered that her appendix had ruptured and poisonous liquids were spreading throughout her body. The doctor administered medicine to help alleviate Junie's pain, but for the next few days, she suffered a high fever and was barely coherent. She then went into a coma for nearly a week. Doctors told my father and Patrinella to expect the worst. Our interim mom stayed at the hospital all week to be with Junie while she suffered.

In the evening of her sixth day in the hospital, the young girl awoke and began to talk and look around the room. Patrinella, who had drifted off, startled at the sound of her sister's voice.

"Did you see that?" Junie asked.

"See what?" replied Patrinella as she wiped the sleep from her eyes.

Speaking in Polish, Junie said she saw "babcia i dziadek"—her grandparents, and they were smiling because they knew she would be joining them soon in heaven. "They were right here in the room," she said. "Didn't you hear me talking to them?"

"No, sweetie, I didn't."

"They told me it's soooo beautiful in heaven and that's where I'll be going," she endured. "The sky is a pretty shade of pink and the temperature is nice and warm. It's just perfect."

Because they passed away thirteen years earlier, Junie had never met her grandparents. She only knew what they looked like from a wedding photo that my family kept on display at the house.

Moments later, my father entered the room. With a big smile on her face, Junie asked if he could hear the beautiful music and see the pretty birds that awaited her in heaven. "No, I can't," he replied as tears rolled down his rugged face.

Junie gently closed her eyes. In a matter of seconds, she stopped breathing.

My father summoned a priest that often made rounds at the hospital and told him what his daughter had said. The priest asked my father if Junie had received her first holy communion. Since she hadn't, the priest administered the sacrament in her hospital room. My father and Patrinella dressed my sister in a beautiful white lace communion dress for the occasion.

When my father came home from the hospital, he put his arm around me and said that Junie had gone to heaven to be with the angels. I cried my eyes out. Four years old at the time, I will always remember that day as the saddest of my childhood.

Doctors at the River Pines Sanatorium permitted my mother to attend the wake and funeral for her daughter, after which she returned to her tuberculosis quarantine.

Buried in her communion dress, Junie never looked prettier. A sad experience for the entire Hintz family, my sister's death left a huge void in my life. The heartbreaking tragedy went a long way in helping me become a man of faith.

A Miracle from God?

As a teenager, my sister Lucille had aspirations of becoming a nun. During the three years my mother was in the sanatorium with tuberculosis, Helena Prusak,* the Polish nurse who cared for her, befriended Lucille. When my mother returned home, the nurse, accompanied by a nun, Sister Mary, would visit our house every two weeks to see how my mother was faring. Lucille would talk to Helena and Sister Mary at length about their chosen professions. Having a positive influence on my sister, they suggested to my parents that they take her to the Sisters of St. Joseph Convent in Stevens Point to help steer her in the direction of nunhood. "She talks about it, dreams about it, and prays about it," said the nun. "It sounds like this is her calling."

As expected, my deeply religious parents were supportive of the idea. To have a nun in the family would be quite an honor. So they took Lucille to the convent where she met the mother superior. She and my parents made the decision that my sister would enroll at St. Joseph where she completed her education and training at the age of sixteen.

At age eighteen, Lucille was allocated to Saint Michael's to assist the Sisters of St. Joseph in caring for patients. In late August 1955, her first assignment was to offer spiritual support to Joe Gavinski, a nineteen-year-old man critically injured in a car accident. Connected to life support, Joe had been in a coma for three weeks. During that time, Lucille would sit with him, hold his hand, and pray for him. But due to the man's condition, doctors told her that his chance for survival was less than 1 percent. So they began discussing a date at which they would disconnect his life support equipment.

The night before the disconnection date, when it appeared all hope was lost, Lucille knelt down next to Joe's bed and prayed to God to spare the man and allow him to wake up from his coma. If He would allow it, she promised to take care of him for the rest of her life. The following day she came to the hospital to see Joe but found that he wasn't in his room. The nurses said they transferred him to a different room because he miraculously awoke from his coma during the night. Lucille was able to talk with Joe over the next few days and told him how happy she was that he was doing better. Three weeks later Joe was able to return home, and Lucille turned her attention to helping other patients.

Several weeks later, the diocesan bishop arrived at Stevens Point to oversee Lucille take her vows of nunhood. Prior to doing so, she was to have a one-hour individual consultation with the bishop to ensure that this was her desired vocation. When he spoke with Lucille, she told him the story of how Joe was in a coma due to his accident and the promise she made to God that if He allowed the man to live she would take care of him for the rest of her life. The bishop, stunned by Lucille's story, refused to let her take her vows. He explained that the promise she made to God was a responsibility she was obliged to fulfill. "You prayed for a miracle," the bishop told her, "and God answered your prayers. Now it's time for you to uphold your end of the deal. You must marry Joe and raise his children. That is your calling." After looking forward to having a nun in the family my parents were in tears.

Shortly after his recovery, Joe visited Lucille at our farmhouse to thank her for her prayers and support, unaware of the pact she made with God. It was then that she spoke to him about her promise.

One year later, Joe and Lucille married and went on to have five daughters. Lucille, who suffered from Lupus, died at the age of forty-four after a massive heart attack.

The Hangover from Hell

In 1958 when I was twelve years old, my two cousins from Chicago paid a visit to our farm. My fourteen-year-old cousin Vern, a bit mischievous, asked me if we had anything to drink. I took him to the cellar and showed him a two-quart jar of dandelion wine that my mother had made. Vern reached up and took it from the shelf. We then drank every last drop of the wine straight from the jar. It was the first time I had ever consumed alcohol. "This is how a boy becomes a man," Vern said with an impish grin. The ensuing hangover, which caused me to puke my guts out, lasted three full days. I had never felt sicker in my life.

Supply and Demand

My grandparents often told me stories of how they lived off the land in the early 1900s before their seven children were born. Even though they maintained a small dairy farm their property was mostly swamp and woods. My grandfather Frank would have my grandmother Helen sit on a tree stump at a crossing where snowshoe hare often scampered. She would shoot the critters as they came by in the cross tracks while he was out poaching deer or trapping beaver and timber wolf. By themselves, the beavers afforded a good living for my grandfather because their pelt was in fashion. At that time, the price of a pelt was a dollar per inch measured from top to bottom and left to right. Each pelt would bring him in upwards of $200—a lot of money back then, particularly for two people trying to make a living from a small farm. He also sold timber wolf pelt for about $100 each, as their fur was in great demand during the frosty northern winters.

In December 1985, I took what I learned from my grandfather and did some beaver trapping to see what I could get for the pelts on the open market. The average profit on each of my thirty-five pelts was $35, a far cry from what my grandfather made nearly seventy-five years before.

Memories of My Father

When a father gives to his son, both laugh;
when a son gives to his father, both cry.
—William Shakespeare

John Hintz, a real tough guy, hated to be called "Daddy." Too feminine, he said. He preferred "Pop." Seeing that he was much bigger than me there was no reason to argue.

In my younger years, if I wanted to ride along with my father on the tractor (a common occurrence) he would simply reach down and with one hand pick me up by the back of my shirt. He would then lift me off the ground and into his lap with little effort.

About once a month, my mother would make fresh loaves of bread brushed generously with butter. My father, eagerly awaiting his favorite treat, would sit at the kitchen table while the bread was still warm and eat an entire loaf with two sticks of butter. He would take a bite of bread and then take a bite off the butter stick devouring everything in one sitting. He would finish the meal with a small cup of tapioca pudding, his favorite dessert.

As my parents neared retirement in the early 1970s my father filed for social security. At the time, they still had the farm, but all that remained were three cows and a few acres of crops. Consequently, my mother and father were struggling financially. On a cool autumn morning in September 1971, my father paid a visit to my house in Plover.

"Son, I need to ask you for a favor," he said as we sat down to talk at the kitchen table. "I need to borrow $60 so I can pay the electric bill."

"No, Pop," I said. "You're not going to borrow the money you're going to take it as a gift. Don't worry about paying it back."

My father, seldom, if ever, an emotional man, looked like he was trying to hold back tears.

"In return I want you to promise me one thing," I said.

"What's that?"

"I want you to allow me to help you to get at least part of the farm sold so you and mom can start living well."

Knowing it was the best thing to do, he agreed.

After a ton of paperwork and preparation, my father sold the family farm in May 1974.

On the evening of Sunday, December 6, 1987, I made the twenty-five-mile trip to see my father who had been ill of late. "Will you please have a drink with me, son?" my father asked. *What the heck is going on,* I thought, *my father rarely drinks?* So I helped him out of bed and led him to his favorite chair. "Mix me a strong one," he said. Though rarely consumed in our house my mother always kept an assortment of libations on hand in the event of company. When my father did decide to imbibe his drink of choice was a tall glass of 7Up with a shot of peppermint schnapps. So I mixed him one, grabbed a can of Pabst Blue Ribbon from the refrigerator, and then sat with him to have a father and son talk. As we chatted, my father grabbed his head several times due to severe headaches.

A few minutes into our conversation my father said, "Nadszedł czas, aby kąpać"—"It's time to bathe" in Polish. I thought it strange since my father was never crazy about water. He seldom, if ever, bathed.

"Are you serious, Pop?"

"Yes, son, I am," he replied. "Will you help me?"

"Of course I will."

Rather weak at age eighty-seven my father would lean forward and nearly fall to the ground when he tried to stand up. "I'm going to help Pop take a shower!" I yelled out to my mother.

"Really?" she said in a surprised tone. My mother knew something was up.

With my arm around his shoulders, I helped my father walk to the bathroom—a converted pantry that housed a small tub and shower—and then helped him disrobe. Looking uncomfortable under the streaming water, he began to lather up with soap. Deep down inside he knew his time was near.

When my father finished his shower, he dried off with an old towel my mother had placed on the chair. He then put on his nightclothes. "Help me get into bed," he said. I then sat there in the room and talked to him a little more. "I think it's my time," he spoke softly as he tried unsuccessfully to raise his head from his pillow.

"What makes you think that, Pop?"

"I saw Momma and Poppa," he said, "last night and again this morning."

"Where did you see them?"

"Last night both of their heads were sticking through the wall smiling at me," he replied. "But this morning it was just Poppa's head I saw. He extended his arm to me and said it was time to go."

"Really?"

"Yes, son."

"So how long do you think you have, Pop?"

"Two days, maybe."

"Are you prepared?"

"Yes, I am. I've already said my 200 rosaries."

"Does dying scare you?" I asked. "Are you afraid?"

"Afraid of what?" he answered. "I'm not afraid of anything, not the least of which death. I'm just going to let nature take its course. We all have to die sometime, don't we?"

Looking at my father, I was proud as could be. Strong and stubborn he was determined to die on his own terms. "Besides," he said, "the one advantage to dying is that you only have to do it once."

John Hintz passed away on December 10, 1987. He was talking in his bedroom with his twenty-one-year-old granddaughter, Renée, who had just flown to Wisconsin from California. He took his last breath while holding her hand, as an ear-to-ear smile remained on his face.

Although an autopsy revealed that my father suffered from a B-12 deficiency, and, perhaps, prostate cancer, the actual cause of his death was never determined.

In 2007, a fire destroyed the old Hintz family farmhouse. My parents, long deceased by then, hadn't lived there for years. What little remained of the dwelling was razed by neighbors.

Lessons from the Farm

There is a certain sense of pride that comes with being raised in a place where hard work, love of family, and unconditional faith were the orders of the day. I wouldn't trade a thing for the lessons I learned while growing up. Lessons such as:

❖ The importance of daily prayer. I prayed for things that most children wouldn't even think about: Rain during a drought, a bountiful harvest, and sunshine when it was time to do my outside chores.

❖ Attending church because we knew we were at the mercy of God. My father taught me to respect God's precious earth because a person is never as close to it as he is on a farm.

❖ Being grateful for the opportunity to behold more sunrises and sunsets than most children my age.

❖ My parents teaching me manners while stressing the importance of respecting my elders. It compelled me to listen and follow instructions without agitation or argument.

❖ Accepting the fact that the older I got the more chores and responsibilities I was given. I wasn't "overworked" or "a slave to my parents." At an early age, my parents taught me responsibility—one of the most valuable lessons a child can learn.

❖ Understanding the value of hard work, commitment, and dedication. Farming is laborious, but deep down inside I knew it would benefit me for the rest of my life.

❖ The importance of family, staying true to your roots, and how determination can inspire a person to accomplish anything, no matter what life has in store.

Farm life was a precious gift that I will always treasure. It was hard work, but I wouldn't want to grow up any other way.

2
School
Days

The difference between school and life?
In school, you're taught a lesson and then given a test.
In life, you're given a test that teaches you a lesson.
—Tom Bodett

Roughly two miles from our farm was the one-room school I attended as a young boy. Polk Elementary employed only two teachers, John Essex and Ethel Duranceau, who taught eight grades in one room with each grade having four students who were assigned a tiny desk. Each grade was called to a large table at the front of the room for its lessons while the rest of the students sat at their desks and worked on assignments.

A wood-burning stove that provided the only heat for the schoolhouse barely put a dent in the chill of a Wisconsin winter. The students carried in wood from a nearby woodshed and then stoked the fire on a rotating basis as assigned by the teacher.

Academically, I was an average student in grade school. The reasons being that I didn't have too much time left to do homework after completing all of my farm chores and the fact that I just plain hated homework.

"Where's Norbert?"

John Essex, also the school disciplinarian at Polk Elementary, would punish any misbehaved students by smacking their butts with a three-inch-wide leather belt. Being rather naughty in my adolescent years, Essex used the belt on me more times than I care to remember.

One of those times, however, was on October 14, 1955 when a classmate of mine, Norbert Wierzba, snuck a recurve bow and broadhead arrows onto the schoolyard. As my brother Jacob climbed a maple tree during recess, Norbert decided to scare him by shooting an arrow into the branches. But he shot a little too close and the blade caught Jacob's calf muscle causing a blood-splattering gash. In my brother's defense, I ran Norbert down, held him by the neck, and then grabbed a piece of rope that was lying close by on the ground. The kid put up quite a fight, but I was able to tie the rope around his ankles and pull him up into the tree where I left him hanging upside down. Moments later the school bell rang and the students returned to class.

"Where's Norbert?" Essex asked.

None of the kids said anything. But the disciplinarian happened to see me sitting at my desk with red cheeks and a shit-eating grin on my face.

Suspecting that something was up Essex took two eighth graders outside with him to look for Norbert. They found him hanging from the tree about ten feet off the ground. Nearly all of the boy's blood had rushed to his head and he was almost unconscious.

Returning to the classroom the disciplinarian took off his leather belt and slowly walked toward me.

"Bend over and put your hands on the potbelly stove!" he ordered.

As punishment for my misdeed, he swung the belt back and landed fifteen lashes on my butt. It took two full days for the pain to go away making it uncomfortable to sit. I didn't dare go home and tell my parents what happened. That would have resulted in fifteen more belt lashes, only this time from my father.

Back then, teachers were the boss. If you were guilty of misbehavior, they would hold it over your head by threatening to inform your parents forcing you to behave going forward.

In time, Norbert would forgive my shenanigans, and we went on to become great friends.

Snake in the Class

Less than a week later, I caught a long, thick pine snake that was trying to slither under the Polk schoolhouse.

Knowing that Mr. Essex hated snakes, it gave me an idea. I took the creature inside where the teacher was quietly correcting homework at his desk while the other students were outside during recess. Carefully, I slid the snake under his desk and crawled away without making a sound. In a matter of seconds, the snake made its way on top of the desk staring Essex square in the face. The teacher let out a terrifying scream as he jumped up from his chair and ran across the classroom.

"Daniel!" he yelled, knowing instantly who was responsible.

Again, I found myself on the wrong end of the disciplinarian's wide leather belt. He bent me over the potbelly stove to administer fifteen more lashes to my behind as punishment.

A Humble Tribute to
the Man in Black

One of the hardest things I had to do in the third grade was to entertain parents during a school Christmas party. The teacher, Mrs. Duranceau, pulled me aside and said that like my fellow classmates I was required to perform something on stage. Unsure of what I wanted to do she decided it might be best for me to sing a song. The song I chose was "Ring of Fire," a top hit from Johnny Cash. From the depths of my family's musty basement, my father retrieved an old junior guitar with five nylon strings, two of which were broken, to play along with the song.

Rather shy at the age of nine, it was difficult for me to ascend Polk Elementary's makeshift stage and "perform" in front of a large crowd. Nonetheless, I was able to find the courage. I put on an old felt hat that the school frequently used as a stage prop and somehow managed to sing Johnny's song, squeaky voice and all. I couldn't get off that stage fast enough. The parents in attendance gave me a standing ovation but it was probably because my face was red with embarrassment.

The Poetry Man or
A Painful Case of Puppy Love

An awkward admission, I used to write little poems when I was in school. I would then pass them along to the cute girls in my class that I had crushes on.

The poems, modestly written, typically proved ineffective. One such body of work…

Roses are red, violets are blue
Sugar is sweet, and so are you
In a matter of time, you will be mine!

…caused the freckled, red-haired girl that I gave it to (who happened to sit behind me in class) to jab in me in the butt with a sharp lead pencil. It really hurt. Even drew some blood. *So much for* that *girl,* I thought.

An Early Lesson in Driving

Mrs. Duranceau had big open sores on her legs due to circulation problems caused by diabetes. A painful condition, the sores often made it difficult for her to walk or drive a car.

In April 1958, Polk Elementary had a softball game scheduled against Mc-Lellan, one of our rivals, about five miles away. But Mrs. Duranceau was in too much pain to drive our team there. The sixty-three-year-old woman, who always regarded me as a teacher's pet, approached me sporting an agonizing grimace. "Do you know how to get to the ball field?" she asked. "Yes, I do," I answered. As a look of relief crossed her face, she handed me the keys to her 1950 Nash Rambler and said, "Okay, get us there!"

With the entire softball team stuffed in the car, including three kids who rode in the trunk with their legs hanging out, I drove us to the game. A little scared that I might hit a streetlamp, or another car, or a pedestrian, I drove along at 25 miles per hour. The Rambler's gears suffered a great deal of grinding, but I got us there safely. Sadly, our team went on to lose the game in embarrassing fashion—20-0. When it was over, I drove everyone back to Polk.

On our arrival, Mrs. Duranceau took me aside and made me promise that I would never tell a soul about driving her car—a promise I had no problem keeping.

Accidents Happen

In the early 1960s, I attended high school in the tiny community of Rosholt, population 610. Thankfully, bus transportation was available since it was a thirteen-mile walk to the school.

Our lunch program cost fifty cents per day. But since school lunches become boring after a while, my friends and I would often leave during our lunch period and walk to Golden's Restaurant where we could buy a hamburger and French fries for the same fifty cents. It was quite a treat to hang out with friends and take walks with our girlfriends.

In a small town, high school students are typically on their own when it comes to finding fun things to do, such as parties with my friends that consisted of a six-pack or two of beer and several packs of cigarettes when we hung out at Bass Lake. After imbibing, we often ended up at Golden's for a plate of greasy fries in an effort to sober up before we went home. On the way to the restaurant after one such party, one of my friends, Maynard Guretski, became sick after pounding too many beers. So the driver of the car parked on a side street in Rosholt and Maynard got out to vomit. While doing so he lowered his head using his hands to brace himself against the passenger's-side door and the rest of us got out of the car to make sure he was okay. But when the last guy to exit the car shut the door Maynard stopped vomiting to let out a hair-raising scream. The car door had slammed his fingers to where they were mashed flat. I lugged my inebriated friend back into the car and the driver rushed him to Saint Michael's for injury treatment. The rest of us then caught a ride home with one of the other guys.

Maynard arrived at school on Monday with metal supports on his three broken fingers. We laughed about it, as good friends do, and even mimicked his screams from the night it happened. I still feel a tingle when I think about how painful it must have been.

3
Leaving Home

Leaving home in a sense involves a kind of
second birth in which we give birth to ourselves.
—Robert Neelly Bellah

Shantytown was a place that I loved. It was home. Filled with humble houses and rustic taverns, it personified quintessential small-town America. But growing up in such a tiny town had its challenges, leaving me with a desire to see what lay beyond its borders. So I left home at the age of eighteen to seek out a life for myself. In the spring of 1964, after doing without for so many years, I moved to Milwaukee—"The Big City"— to find full-time work and settle into a new way of life.

Culture Shock

Arriving in Milwaukee, I was amazed at how different it was from my tiny hometown. Moving to a city of half a million people was like walking onto another planet. The hustle and bustle of the metropolis was unlike anything I had experienced; completely different from the quiet, secluded life I lived in the countryside of central Wisconsin.

I couldn't believe how city people lived as opposed to those raised on a farm. When city people ran out of food, they went to the grocery store. When farm people ran out of food they went to the basement and pulled a few Mason jars off the shelf or went outside to the fields and slaughtered an animal.

Working for a Living

The first thing I did upon moving to Milwaukee was apply for work at Unit Drop Forge in West Allis about six miles west of the city. As I filled out the paperwork, the hiring manager showed me a stack of completed applications more than a foot high. He then asked where I was from. "Marathon County, sir," I replied. Immediately, he placed my application at the top of the stack. "You people out there really know how to work," he said. The following week I was hired.

The job was physically demanding, but it paid one of the highest wages in the Milwaukee area. I couldn't believe the size of my first paycheck. It was bigger than any farm-related check my father ever earned. To someone who had spent his entire life laboring on a farm, working a 9-5 job was a terrific way of life. My coworkers thought it was tough but to me it was more like a part-time job. After eight hours, I was able to punch out! I was off on Saturdays and Sundays! Plus, I got holidays off with pay! What more could a young man ask for?

After six months, I had enough money saved to buy a 1955 Oldsmobile convertible. Still, the freedom to come and go as I pleased was a transition that took several months to get used to. Eventually, I grew accustomed to meeting girls, seeing movies at indoor theaters, and hanging out with friends at White Tower restaurants.

Unit Drop Forge had twelve colossal 8,000-pound dropforging hammers that pounded white-hot steel into shape. This was done in a two-foot-high furnace with sliding doors through which I loaded the steel. The foundry made products ranging from end bits for graders to four cylinder crankshafts weighing close to 500 pounds. My job was to heat the furnace to 2,250 degrees and then swing 150-pound pieces of steel over to one of the steam-powered hammers when they were ready. For safety's sake, I wore earplugs, earmuffs, and a helmet with a hinged plexiglass face guard. The tinted goggles I wore underneath allowed me to look into the furnace without damaging my eyes. By the end of my shift, the face guard had warped from the heat of the furnace to where I could barely see out of it.

The steam-powered hammers at Unit Drop Forge were so powerful that the foundry had to pay for basement repairs in many of the homes surrounding it, some as far away as three blocks. One evening after work, I went out to shoot pool with my friends in a tavern located four blocks away. We couldn't get the billiard balls to stay still on the table due to the reverberations caused by the hammers.

The temperature inside the foundry was often unbearably hot, making the arduous labor I performed for my wages that much tougher. In the summer, when thermometers outside were topping 90 degrees, the temperature inside would rise to about 140 degrees; so hot that workers would take salt tablets by the handfuls to stave off dehydration. Since the foundry didn't have air-conditioning, management would allow workers to punch out and take occasional breaks to cool off. The water bubblers in and around the foundry were maintained at room temperature so no one would die of shock from drinking ice-cold water.

Ironically, the clothing I wore to perform my job appeared more suitable for winter weather. Largely wool based and rather uncomfortable, I sported long johns under Levi blue jeans with a thermal undershirt beneath a long-sleeve shirt. Working in close proximity to hot steel made this wardrobe necessary to keep the extreme heat from cooking my skin.

Just Wanted to Hang Out with Friends

In September 1964, I decided to visit some friends in Stevens Point and join them in having a beer or two at Romy's Rendezvous, a local watering hole. While standing at the bar talking there happened to be a woman sitting to my right. I had no idea that the woman was there with her boyfriend, Zach Biel,* who, at the time, was shooting pool. In close proximity to the woman, Zach, a few years my senior, thought I was trying to hit on her. So he sauntered over to where I was standing and tapped me on the shoulder. When I turned to face him, he swung his right arm around with a Coke bottle in his hand. The bottle struck under my bottom lip driving four of my upper front teeth into my skull. Had the bottle hit me a quarter inch closer I would have been dead since he likely would have driven my nose into my brain.

Somewhat dazed, I prepared to go a few rounds with Zach when one of my friends grabbed me from behind. "Go to the men's room and look in the mirror," he said. I saw that my bottom lip was hanging by a thread ready to fall off at any second. I could actually stick my tongue through the hole between my bottom lip and my upper chin. Blood covered almost every inch of my T-shirt and jeans. When I returned to the crowded bar I noticed several patrons had been splashed with my blood including a girl wearing a white skirt and matching top sitting on a barstool. She was drenched from head to toe. Zach and his girlfriend, meanwhile, were nowhere to be found.

Several weeks later, my friends and I searched the neighborhood bars for the man responsible for my injury. But the locals informed us that shortly after the incident he left town for parts unknown. Several people believed he was still somewhere in Wisconsin, while others said he moved as far away as Florida. Either way, Zach was gone.

To this day, my lip still bears a scar from the incident.

Racial Tensions in Milwaukee

Just south of the viaducts in Milwaukee, a five-block-wide neighborhood served as a buffer between the blacks and the predominantly Polish white community; in particular, a strip of land along National Avenue over to Greenfield mostly populated by Hispanics. For the most part, the Hispanic community got along with the whites, but not with the blacks. The Hispanics hated the blacks. Trouble always existed between the two communities. But there was also frequent trouble between the blacks and the whites.

On a chilly night in October 1964, I was hanging out with a couple of guys at the White Tower restaurant on Mitchell Street in Milwaukee. The men, who I met just a few months earlier, would gather twice a week at the restaurant—a popular soda fountain-style hamburger joint of the era. One of the guys, "Tiny" Tim Kulczycki,* a 6-foot-7, 350-pound man, was sitting next to me at the restaurant counter making small talk. As I watched Tiny pull a flask from his jacket and spike his soda with whiskey, a funny, wisecracking fellow named Jerry walked through the door. Short in size and light in weight, perhaps 5 foot 7, 150 pounds, he strolled over to where we were sitting.

"Hey, Tiny!" he yelled.

"Don't you see I'm talking to someone," Tiny said.

"Hey, Tiny!" the little man yelled once more.

Annoyed, my mammoth friend turned around on his rotating counter stool. Facing Jerry, he extended his right arm, picked the guy up by his jacket, and lifted him off the floor.

"I told you not to bother me when I'm talking!" he bellowed.

Tiny then turned his focus back to me. "Now, where were we?" he asked as Jerry's feet dangled about a foot above the restaurant floor.

Just then, four men wearing leather jackets walked into the restaurant. The men, whom I didn't know, walked up to Tiny and one of them slapped the counter in front of him. As it turned out, the guys were friends of Tiny and he had asked them to meet him at the restaurant. There happened to be a black-themed movie—*Black Like Me,* if my memory stands correct—playing at the theater across the street. A group of black men and women had driven there in separate cars from the north side of Milwaukee, parking in the big lot behind the theater. From the restaurant window, Tiny watched intently as the blacks walked into the theater. He then returned his attention back to his burger and spiked soda. About an hour and a half later, he pointed his finger at Jerry and said, "Go across the street and find out what time the movie lets out." The little man sprinted to the theater and then sprinted back. "In about ten minutes or so," he said. "Okay guys, get in your places," Tiny commanded with an evil grin on his face. The four leather-clad men ran behind the theater to an unlit part of the parking lot, retrieved the tire irons they had stashed in their cars, and proceeded to stake out where they couldn't be seen. Then they waited in anticipation for the long line of black patrons that would soon exit the movie. Among the first to do so were four young black men who walked around the corner of the building to the back lot. Tiny's friends beat them senseless with their tire irons before they could get into their cars. I heard screams emanating from behind the theater, then the sounds of two cars peeling off in different directions. Within minutes, sirens began to blare. My huge friend just sat in his seat smiling while staring intently out the restaurant window.

"What the hell is going on out there?" I asked Tiny, unaware of what was transpiring. "Nothing," he replied. "Just enjoy your soda." Moments later, the leather-clad men walked back into the restaurant. "So, did you place our orders yet?" they asked as if nothing had happened. Looking outside the restaurant window, I saw several squad cars surround the theater as medical workers loaded the beaten and bloodied black men into ambulances. No one from the Milwaukee Police Department entered the restaurant to question anyone and no arrests were ever made.

After that night, I stopped hanging around Tiny and his inner circle. It was time to find new friends.

It's worth noting that for most of 1964, I hung around a tough bunch of guys.

It was 3 A.M. on a cool, early morning in September when my friends John Chudzik,* Will Jesko,* Greg Makosky,* and I were riding around Milwaukee killing time. John, who owned the car, blurted, "I could use a smoke." So we pulled into a liquor store parking lot to pick up a pack of cigarettes from a vending machine sitting outside. John pumped his quarters into the machine but it didn't spit out any smokes. He then kicked it three times, but to no avail. With a look of anger on his face, he grabbed the machine with both hands and knocked it over. He went into the trunk of his car and pulled out a rope tying one end of it to the trunk and the other end to the machine. John then gunned the accelerator and sped away. The faulty cigarette machine dragging behind, it bounced up and down on the street as packs of smokes and pieces of glass and metal went flying everywhere. Sitting in the back seat of the car watching it unfold I was scared to death that someone could do something like this. John drove about three blocks and then turned into an alley. He untied the machine, shoved it into the trunk of his car, and then drove to a park. My friend then reached through the broken glass on the face of the machine, grabbed a pack of cigarettes, and was finally able to have the smoke he so badly wanted.

Afterward, I started hanging out with several guys from Stevens Point and Marathon County who, like me, had moved to Milwaukee. One of them ended up sharing an apartment with me in the city. This was also around the time that I met a young lady named Shirley and fell in love.

The rest, as they say, is history.

PART TWO
THE MILITARY

4
SERVING
THE U.S.A.

Ask not what your country can do for you,
ask what you can do for your country.
—John F. Kennedy

The values of serving in the U.S. military are self-evident: Upholding allegiance to the Constitution, your branch, your unit, and other soldiers; fulfilling your obligations beyond your assigned tasks; treating people with dignity and respect; putting the safety of your nation, the military, and your dependents before your own; being honorable in every choice you make and doing what's right by adhering to ethical principles. Not to mention developing personal courage in the face of danger or fear.

Many Americans know the definitions of the words Duty, Honor, Integrity, Loyalty, Personal Courage, Respect, and Selfless Service. But to personify them is something entirely different. They are the Seven Core Army Values learned by soldiers during Basic Training abided by in daily life in everything they do, whether personal or professional.

Family Influence

While serving in the Marine Corps at Camp Pendleton, California, my eldest brother Sylvester was summoned to the Lebanon crisis in 1958. But the ordeal was settled before his ship landed and he didn't have to face live action.

After boot camp, Sylvester came home on his first leave in July 1958 to visit the family. In full uniform and powerfully built, his transition from boy to man was awe-inspiring. When my brother wore his uniform to church and family functions, I felt special just being around him. Seeing him so physically fit made quite an impression on me. I also admired how tough he had become.

During his visit, Sylvester stopped by Chet's Tavern in Shantytown to hang out with some old friends. While having a beer, he encountered Albert Plonka,* a local man with a reputation for bar fights. Sure enough, they ended up brawling. My brother took Albert on his shoulder and ran him head first through a wall of bread shelves, the tavern doubling as a convenience store and drinking establishment. The fight was over as quickly as it started.

The following day my father and I went to the store portion of the tavern with sacks of cucumbers given that the establishment also acted as a receiving station. We dumped the sacks into a large sorting machine since payment for the vegetables was relative to their size. When we walked into the tavern area to receive our check we witnessed Sylvester sitting at the bar with the man he had driven through the wall. Side by side, they had their arms around each other as they drank cold draft beers. My brother had earned the bully's unconditional respect.

Admiring Sylvester's strength and will, I knew that I wanted to be just like him.

Getting Started

Residing in the Milwaukee area served me well. Not only was I earning a great living at Unit Drop Forge I also met Shirley, the woman who would become my wife. I was nineteen years old when we married on October 7, 1965. Shirley was almost twenty-one.

Yet as I recalled memories of Sylvester, there remained a part of me that wanted to serve my country. So in September 1965, I paid a visit to my local Army recruiting office to speak with a representative. Though hardly in a position to dictate terms, I informed him that I was to marry Shirley in October and it would be nice to be home for our first Christmas together. He explained that the only way it could be achieved would be to file for a deferment due to my impending marital status. Since I wasn't interested in avoiding my duty to serve in the military, I asked if there was any other way. He told me that a group of recruits was leaving for Fort Knox, Kentucky on October 14 and if I would volunteer the draft, he could assign me to that group.

The deal was sealed.

After receiving draft papers, I met with my Army recruiter who promised I would be home for Christmas. At the conclusion of basic training, I would receive a ten-day leave starting on December 23 and then report to Advanced Individual Training (AIT).

Life in the U.S. Army

For soon-to-be soldiers, the first day at Fort Knox meant orientation and uniform measurement. After height and weight were recorded, two sets of fatigues labeled "medium" were tossed at us followed by caps and boots of identical size with no chance to try them on. Next, we received two towels, two bars of soap, and a washcloth along with three pairs of socks. Then came the platoon assignment along with a bunk bed and footlocker. Shortly after, we were off to the barbershop where six recruits equipped with large electric hair clippers stood at the ready. Our haircuts, which took about two minutes while sitting on empty five-gallon buckets, were all the same—five times across the skull with the clippers and it was over. When it was time to hit the showers, two men with garden hoses sprayed us down with a disinfectant before we were able to turn on the water. Then we shaved, went to our barracks to get dressed, and learned the proper way to make a bed. After that, it was out to practice formation and back to the mess hall to study and recite the military code of conduct. At 10 P.M., it was time for bed.

Reveille Comes Early

At 4:30 A.M., a restful sleep was shattered by reveille, trumpeted with a discomforting blare into the ears of every young soldier. We were given thirty minutes to make our bunks, shower and shave, dress, and fall into formation. The drill instructor then walked between the rows of men inspecting uniforms while asking each of us to recite the code of conduct. Those that got it wrong became accustomed to the military push up; similar to a standard push up, but with elbows pinned tightly against your sides to exert more pressure on the triceps.

We would then arrive at the mess hall. While standing in line for our breakfast we exercised—push-ups, pull-ups, and running in place. After eating, it was Physical Training and a marching drill. We ran on a five-mile circular track to the rifle range and marched back for a quick lunch. More drills were followed by the Physical Training course, which consisted of one hundred push-ups and sit-ups, horizontal bars, and low crawl—pulling with your elbows and pushing with your legs for 120 meters. Soldiers were instructed to hold their rifles across their arms not allowing them to touch the dirt on their stomachs. After running five more miles, we reported to the mess hall for dinner and then performed dismount drills until 8 P.M. When we finished, it was back to the barracks to clean up, shower and shave, polish equipment, and prepare for inspection. At 10 P.M., it was lights out. It continued this way, seven days a week for eight weeks. On Sunday at 10 A.M. after Physical Training, we marched to church service. After church, it was more of the same.

The true physical test came during the first week of December: a twenty-two mile march that resulted in so many massive, throbbing blisters on my feet there was nary an inch of room for another. The march, conducted from 6 A.M. until midnight, was followed by the infiltration course—crawling in mud under barbed wire fence in total darkness with machine guns shooting four feet above you. If you stood up you were dead. Every fifth round was a tracer with white streaks looking as if they were coming right at you. We rolled off a concrete base at the beginning of the course and then crawled through aprons with and without a rifle. When you crawled with the rifle, you positioned it between the ground and your chest and you slid underneath the barbed wire, which was about a foot off the ground. You used the rifle to slide on so you could go through faster. We then ran a half circle into the next bay of bunkers filled with sandbags that had timed detonators containing explosives. As we crawled through them, it was pitch dark, so you had to feel your way through. When you felt a sandbag, you would drop your head because you knew it was going to blast.

Next, was live hand grenade training. We lobbed the grenades into truck tires lying flat on the ground, which served as targets. If your grenade fell inside the tire, you passed. If you missed, you practiced throwing every time the platoon was afforded a break. The purpose of the intense training was to push you to your maximum potential without breaking your spirit.

Not helping matters was the fact that I smoked during my time in the army. I learned how to field strip my cigarettes by opening the paper, flicking out the ashes, and then putting the paper and filter in my pocket. My comrades and I would often take cigarette breaks particularly during long hikes and marches. We also had a "butt brigade" where early each morning at sunrise the soldiers that smoked would take a bag and collect the hundreds of cigarette butts that were lying on the ground.

Despite my dirty habit, after ten weeks of arduous training, I felt ready to take on anything.

The final week of training encompassed physical fitness tests: Dismounted drills with rifles, rifle range testing, and then final inspections by the Inspector General. If all went well you were able to graduate.

My future military training assignment was based on a written exam I took a short time after starting basic training at Fort Knox. There was a segment on Morse code that I passed with flying colors. For that reason, I was assigned a military occupational specialty (MOS) for communications.

Fort Gordon

After graduating basic training, I received orders to report to Fort Gordon, Georgia for AIT. On December 28, 1965, my wife and I packed up our 1959 Chevy Impala and hit the road with $160 in our pockets. Our personal belongings were crammed so tightly in the car they practically burst out of the windows. By the time we hit Georgia two days later, two of the tires on the car had rubber peeling off them. I pulled into an old but still functioning tobacco plantation near the town of Macon where an eighty-something couple, Billy* and Susannah Adcock,* resided. Shirley stayed at the house with Susannah while Billy drove me to several towns to look for two good used tires. When he found a pair he liked he bought them for me and we drove back to the plantation. There, Shirley and Susannah were sitting at the kitchen table talking and eating homemade peach pie with vanilla ice cream. Two of the kindest people I ever met, the Adcocks refused to take any money for the tires or the gas to drive me around. It was southern hospitality at its finest.

Shirley and I arrived at Fort Gordon on December 31 and began searching for a cheap place to live in Augusta, a few miles from the post. We found a tiny one-bedroom cabin next to an auto service station for $60 a month. The cabin had no heat or air conditioning but my wife and I figured it might be the best place we could find for the money. We unloaded our car and began to settle in. While my wife unpacked, I made a trip to a local store to pick up some food for our cabinets. As tired as we were, we decided to hit the hay when I got back. In the middle of the night, my wife awoke to the sound of little clicking noises. When she turned the light on, we witnessed what had to be a hundred or so cockroaches scattering to the cracks and crevices in the walls. I had never seen so many of the little monsters in one place in my entire life. We sprayed the hell out of the apartment and were able to keep them under control, but not before they helped themselves to our food and crawled inside our clothes. I never realized how many cockroaches there were on the property until a few weeks later when we received a night of torrential rain. On waking up in the morning, I noticed that outside the cabin surrounding large puddles of water were potentially thousands of cockroaches, some as big as mice. It looked as if they were drinking water or laying eggs, perhaps both. I started beating them down with a shovel and was able to squash quite a few, but plenty were able to get away. We also had trouble with rats and mice since there were several openings around the drainpipe under our sink. I stuffed at least a dozen scouring pads into the openings to keep the vermin from getting into the cabin.

On the morning of January 3, 1966, I reported to Fort Gordon and met with the company commander to ask permission to live off post with my young wife since she was pregnant. Hesitant at first, the commander granted my request. But in return I had to pull change of quarters (CQ) duty where I ran messages for the commander, picked up mail, and forwarded telephone calls as ordered from midnight to 2 A.M. Six days per week, I was also to attend 72B20 Communications Center Specialist classes on post at Southeastern Signal School from 4 P.M. until midnight before it was time to honor my CQ duty.

Strapped for cash, Shirley and I did whatever we could to make ends meet. My wife used her portable sewing machine to make extra money by repairing and altering fatigues for the men on post. I would do my part by offering the men rides to and from Augusta for a dollar per head. I would stuff as many as seven men into the car at once to maximize profit. The extra money came in handy considering the meager $79 a month in military pay I received.

South Korea

After twelve weeks of AIT at Fort Gordon, I received a promotion to Private First Class (E-3). A few days later, I received orders to Korea. Given two hours to leave post, I returned to my apartment to pack, say goodbye to my wife, and then return to Fort Gordon where I was restricted to post. It gave me time to speak with my landlord who agreed to sell my car for me and forward the money to my wife who was planning to take a bus to Milwaukee. Two days later, I was traveling on a bus to Oakland International Airport in California.

Before arriving in Korea, I was held in Japan at Camp Zama—a U.S. Army post located about twenty-five miles southwest of Tokyo, while my ten-day federal background check was performed. The F.B.I., always thorough, contacted my family in Wisconsin to ask questions about me. My mother was worried sick thinking I was in in trouble with the law. I explained to her that it was simply part of the investigative process.

After receiving clearance, I was able to transfer from Japan to Seoul. I was then assigned to an artillery battalion where I worked in a single room communications center made of concrete surrounded by a sixteen-foot-tall chain-link fence. A short distance from the Demilitarized Zone, I worked twenty-four hours on and twenty-four hours off at the center since there were only two of us with the same MOS. Holding a top-secret crypto clearance, my job was to code and decode messages dealing with military movements. The messages were decoded from a ribbon, then encrypted on the teletype and sent out to their destination. To avoid missing messages we rigged alarms that the carriage on the teletype would strike when it reached the end of the track.

Sacked lunches were delivered to us through a porthole in the gate since the servers didn't have the authority or clearance to enter the enclosure. It was a lonely assignment, but I learned to bide time reading the *Army Times* and writing letters home to my wife and parents.

The standard of living in South Korea was shocking. There were thousands of people living in squalid slums. As far as the eye could see, there were tiny huts with walls made from river clay and straw roofs made from rice thatch woven together tightly to make them as watertight as possible. The huts, built in long rows, had drainage ditches behind them where people typically urinated and defecated. They washed their clothes in muddy rivers by striking and scrubbing them on slime-covered rocks. Their drinking water came from the same rivers. I also witnessed the fly-covered carcasses of dead dogs hanging in the windows of unsanitary shops with no refrigeration. Man's best friend slaughtered for food, ready for consumption by people so poor they weren't above eating dirt. Just the thought of it was enough to turn my stomach.

The majority of the Korean populace wore round, cone-shaped straw hats and pushed two-wheeled carts loaded with Kimchi, a spicy pickled cabbage that happens to be Korea's national dish. Men, women, and children of all ages would stack it in large heaps and let it ferment in the sun. After they ate it, you could smell their breath from a mile away.

Where weather is concerned, South Korea has four well-defined seasons. The country's winter season often gets cold with heavy snow and the summers are hot and wet. The rainfall they receive from monsoons is typically measured in feet rather than inches.

I found it somewhat humorous that if the Koreans didn't like you, they would call you a "fuckin' number ten GI." Rated on a scale from one to ten, being a "one" meant you were well liked, but being a "ten" meant you were loathed.

* * *

Soldiers were housed in batteries rather than barracks inside Quonset huts with cement floors. There were twelve soldiers per billet—six GIs and six Republic of Korea soldiers (ROKs). The money ROKs received for being in the Korean military was equivalent to $1.68 per month in American funds. They also received a monthly care package from the U.S. military containing survival items left over from the Korean War. Arriving in large wooden crates each package contained three pairs of socks, a facial washcloth, a hand towel, several rolls of toilet paper, two bars of soap, a can of shoe polish, chocolate candy bars, and two cartons of cigarettes. At the end of each year, they received a new pair of combat boots, which were all the same size. No matter how big or small the ROKs' feet were those were the boots they were forced to wear. It was "one size fits all" whether they liked it or not.

The monthly care packages also contained K-rations—individual daily combat food (mostly Spam, but occasionally beans with chunks of pork or miniature hotdogs). K-rations provided three separately boxed meal units for breakfast, lunch, and dinner. The food, packaged in metal olive drab (OD)-colored cans, was left over from World War II. At more than twenty years old, the stench of the food caused the American soldiers to turn their heads away to keep from vomiting each time one of the cans was opened. Though hardly appealing, this type of food was loved by the ROKs. They appreciated their care packages for without them it would have been hard to survive.

The rations for the American soldiers out in the field consisted of eggs, milk, and potatoes in powdered form inside sealed bags. The water to mix with them needed to be extremely hot or else a soldier would choke on big, dry lumps of powder.

The liner of the M1 steel pot helmets we wore was made from fiberglass with a headpiece inside of it. Held in place by an elastic OD band, we positioned the two-pound pot helmet over it so it could deflect bullets. The helmet was also practical for cooking and as a toilet for use in a foxhole.

Return to Wisconsin

In July 1966, my battery commander, Joe Bartlett, had me report to his office

At age eight. April 1954

1955: Polk Elementary School near Shantytown in Marathon County. That's me sitting in the second row from the side windows, third student from the front. Behind me in the photo (not the row) is my sister Delphene. At the front of my row is my brother John. Before him with her head resting in her hands is my sister Susan. Standing in the back of the room sporting his mandatory stern look is John Essex, the schoolteacher and disciplinarian.

Bernice "Junie" Hintz
at age eight in 1949

My "miracle" sister Lucille
at age eighteen in 1956

Basic training graduation photo,
December 20, 1965 at Fort Knox, Kentucky

At Camp McCoy after returning from a tour in Korea in July 1966. Responsible for operating the communications center for the army reserve troops, I also helped train more than 30,000 reserves from July 1966-October 1967. From left to right: SGT Daniel V. Hintz, SP4 George V. Bailey, SGT Emil Bakka, and Major Raymond T. Hermanson. Commanding Officer of HHD (5011).

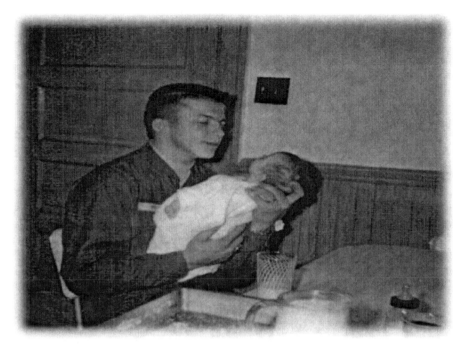

Summer 1966: A proud father holds his "war baby." Danielle Marie Hintz was eight weeks old when I first saw her after returning from South Korea. This was in the apartment Shirley and I rented in Sparta, Wisconsin while I was stationed at Camp McCoy.

Summer 1966, age twenty. Typing a military activity report in our tiny apartment in Sparta because the job didn't stop at the office.

Basic training group graduation, December 20, 1965. Seated in the front row on the far left, I was proud to serve as our squad leader. In the middle of the front row wearing the "Smokey" hat is Sgt. Attaway, the drill instructor—tough as nails, but one hell of a guy.

April 1966: Waiting for the Inspector General to arrive at Camp Santa Barbara in South Korea, not far from the DMZ

June 1966:
My sister Susan's
high school graduation
photo, just short of her
eighteenth birthday.
This photo was taken
only a few weeks before
the accident that would
eventually take her life.

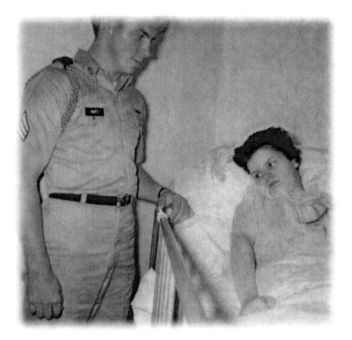

Susan and I were
very close. She would
write to me at least
twice a week while I
was stationed in
Korea. It was
heartbreaking to see
her in this condition.

May 1979: My parents, Bernice and John Hintz, in front of the
Saint Ladislaus Catholic Parish in Bevent on their 50th wedding
anniversary. My mother was seventy years old, my father, seventy-nine.

The brothers Hintz in 1979 outside Saint Ladislaus Catholic Parish
in Bevent. From left to right: John, Sylvester, me, Jacob, Stanley

ASAP saying he had received an urgent telegram from the Red Cross that required my immediate attention. Arriving at once, I learned that my sister Susan had been involved in an auto accident. In a state of comatose, she wasn't expected to live. I was instructed to pack some clothing and personal items and prepare to return to Wisconsin immediately.

Commander Bartlett had a jeep waiting to transport me to Seoul Airport where I boarded an eighteen-hour flight to Tacoma, Washington. When I approached the civilian terminal, I saw that the airline union had walked out on strike and all flights were grounded. I then went to the armed forces airfield about two miles from Tacoma to see if I could get a military hop. The first lieutenant informed me that a four-engine cargo plane would soon be leaving for Detroit, Michigan as soon as it completed its engine tests and inspection. One by one, the crew fired the engines, but when they fired the fourth one, it instantly ignited causing smoke and flames to shoot out of the rear. *Oh my God,* I thought, *I'm never to going to get home.* Moments later, a commander in a flight suit approached me and suggested that I travel with a bomber leaving for Lackland Air Force Base in San Antonio, Texas. I jumped at the chance since from there I could take a civilian flight to Milwaukee.

I arrived home to find Susan in a full coma. Several days before, she had gone out with a friend, Cindy Brodzik,* and my cousin, Steve Lasko,* whom Cindy was dating, to celebrate her eighteenth birthday. The three of them drove in John's car to Staszak's Tavern in Marathon County. After having a few drinks, my sister wanted to go home as it was getting late. Apparently, Steve was getting agitated over her pestering him about leaving. So he gave his keys to the girls and let them use his car.

As the girls drove east on Townline Road, a gravel side street, they turned sharply to the left and control of the car was lost. The vehicle propelled straight ahead and struck an embankment head on ejecting Susan through the windshield and into a hayfield. Cindy, still inside the car, was knocked unconscious. When Marathon County officers arrived with an ambulance about twenty minutes later they found the lifeless woman in the car, but saw no one else around. Cindy was loaded into the ambulance and transported to Wausau Hospital. Regaining consciousness on the way, she immediately started asking for Susan telling the ambulance attendant that she was not alone in the car.

The attendant then radioed the deputies at the accident scene and they began searching the hayfield. They found my sister lying on the ground unconscious with her head twisted under her chest. The doctors at the hospital surmised that her injuries kept her from breathing for too long, which, in turn, caused severe brain damage.

Susan remained in a vegetative state for the rest of her life passing away in 1980, fourteen years after the accident. To this day, it remains unclear as to who was driving the car.

With my family devastated over Susan's accident, I thought it was best to remain in Wisconsin. During my time in Milwaukee, I did what the military always says: "Contact your Congressman." So I called Melvin Laird, and three days later, I received a telegram that he arranged a compassionate re-assignment for me to finish my tour of duty at Camp McCoy, a U.S. Army installation in Monroe County.

During my third week at Camp McCoy, I was summoned to the commander's office to meet with Colonel Craig. Suspecting I was in some kind of trouble, I was shocked when he handed me a large envelope from my battery commander in South Korea. Inside was a document affirming a promotion to Specialist Fourth Class—an unexpected surprise that came with a pay raise!

Two months later, I was promoted to Sergeant E-5 just in time for the influx of summer trainees. I was pleased to hear that with the promotion I was entitled to free, on-post housing. So my wife and I moved into a converted military hospital with three large bedrooms, a kitchen, an indoor laundry room, and a two-car garage—luxury living compared to what we were accustomed to.

During the spring and summer seasons, Camp McCoy was bustling with trainees, but in the winter, those trainees were gone. The post had thirteen permanently assigned GIs, including myself, along with 250 civilian workers. Like one big family, we would get together every weekend at a different apartment for drinks, snacks, and board games.

In August 1966, I became a part-time youth counselor at the Camp McCoy job corps center. Working with delinquent men between the ages of sixteen and twenty-one, my function was to offer guidance to help them return to society as reformed citizens. The job corps center was a federal program much like boot camp and an education facility combined. Young men from all over the country were there instead of serving time in prisons, their charges ranging from petty offenses to burglary and auto theft. The center, sanctioned by Congress to deal with the overpopulation of prisons, was designed to keep less serious offenders from serving potentially lengthy prison sentences.

Several weeks earlier, my wife and I welcomed our first child, a baby girl. After an honorable discharge from the U.S. Army on October 13, 1967, we moved back to Milwaukee where I returned to my old job at Unit Drop Forge. Since the workforce at the foundry enjoyed a strong labor union, my seniority was retained throughout my time in the military.

PART THREE
THE BADGE

5

Deputy Stories

Entering Law Enforcement

My wife, daughter, and I lived in Milwaukee for about a year before moving to the town of Mequon in Ozaukee County roughly nineteen miles to the north. We lived there for two years while I worked my full-time job at Unit Drop Forge. It was in Mequon that I also began fulfilling my dream of working in law enforcement. In December 1967, the Ozaukee County Sheriff's Department, headquartered in Port Washington, hired me as a part-time deputy where I worked until March 1969.

* * *

In the late 1960s, things weren't looking good for civil rights and race relations in America. News coverage was making the nation aware of the ugliness of racism, an impression that would continue into the early 1970s with conflicts over school integration and the murders of several civil rights activists.

While attending the Milwaukee Police Academy to study crime scene investigation I befriended a city police officer. He told me a racially tinged story that has stayed with me to this day.

In 1966 during race-related street protests in Milwaukee, the officer, a hulking 6-foot-4, 330-pound Irishman named Jim Callahan,* was assigned to break in a new recruit while he walked his beat in a rough and tumble part of the city. Walking side by side for about thirty minutes they came across a teenage black man urinating on the side of an office building. Callahan turned to the rookie and told him to take action. He approached the young man and then reached into his back pocket to retrieve his citation book. The officer grabbed his hand and stopped him. "Son, let me show you how it's done out here," he said. He walked up to the black man, seized him by the neck, and shook him violently. Without time to finish his urination and zip his fly, the man's penis was swinging in the wind. "If I ever catch you pissing in public again," Callahan yelled, "I'll send you home with your cock and balls in a paper sack!" The officer then spun the man around. "Now get the hell outta here!" he yelled while kicking him in the ass. He turned to the recruit with a satisfied grin on his face. "That's how we enforce the law in this neck of the woods," he said. "Screw that fuckin' citation book. When you go home tonight, I want you to burn it. You won't be needing it anymore."

This was an unusual situation in that the Milwaukee Police Department during this turbulent era would typically assign a minimum of four officers at a time to patrol the city streets. The reason being that black citizens often sat on the rooftops of local tenement buildings and waited for white police officers to walk their beats on the sidewalks below. They would then drop buckets full of concrete or wet sand on their heads. Several officers were critically injured due to such actions, and there was no way to find out who was responsible. When you walked into one of those buildings there were in upwards of 300 black men, women, and children living inside who refused to talk.

*   *   *

The main corridor in the Milwaukee Police Academy featured a large gold-plated archway that stretched about ten feet across. Inscribed on the front were the words "If it ain't written, it ain't." The Milwaukee Police Department had a policy where on the first day of every month each patrol officer received a leather-bound notebook for recording notes, statistics, and details regarding what went on during that officer's beat. On the last day of every month, the officers had to turn in their notebooks to the police chief and sign for a new one. Everything inside the notebooks was evidence admissible to any court of law at any time.

In April 1969, my mother-in-law mailed me a newspaper clipping from Stevens Point saying the sheriff's department was looking to hire deputies. Thinking this could be my chance to find full-time law enforcement work, I applied immediately. The subsequent processes of screening and testing took two months, but I passed with excellence. On May 1, 1969, I became a Portage County sheriff's deputy.

The job paid $480 per month. Supporting two children at the time, my wife and I bought our first house in Whiting for $12,000 on the G.I. Bill, no down payment needed. We planted our roots and the next chapter of our lives began.

I attended several training academies and trained with senior officers for nearly a year before being assigned to a four-man patrol squad unit that rotated shifts and duties.

As a deputy, I handled the civil process service as well as criminal and bench warrants where the person had to be brought in and booked into the county jail. I also handled emergency mental commitments at night and on weekends when a judge wasn't available. It was my job to respond to traffic accidents, bar fights, domestic disputes, house fires, farm and industrial accidents, burglaries, robberies, and homicides. The work was never ending, always different, and far from boring.

A Ride I'll Never Forget

July 17, 1969

For most of its history, the Wisconsin Highway Commission was in charge of traffic patrol and enforcement until the division merged with the Portage County Sheriff's Department in the late 1950s. In the process, Neil Ketchum, the chief of the Portage County Traffic Patrol, was transferred to the sheriff's department where he worked as a road sergeant. About ten years later, the first assignment I was given was to ride with Neil on patrol before I was allocated my own car. At the time, I was still a little wet behind the ears.

Neil, a large man with a big, protruding gut, always sat sideways while inside his squad car. Hardly comfortable, it was the only way he could fit himself in the driver's seat without the steering wheel poking his stomach. As I rode with the traffic patrol chief on a scorching hot summer day, he pointed out that when driving to an emergency "you need to show more concern to tail lights than to head lights." He pointed out that the greatest threat was the drivers ahead of you being startled by the red lights and siren of a squad car causing them to slam their breaks, and the fact that oncoming traffic can see your emergency lights so you're better off hugging the center line.

Later that day, we received a call about a farm tractor on Highway 54 at County Trunk JJ. While pulling a crop sprayer the tractor was involved in an accident with another vehicle. The ensuing ride to the scene was one I'll never forget. Neil headed south on Business Highway 51 since the accident happened in Buena Vista, south of Plover. Proceeding at a speed of 90 miles per hour, Neil was sitting at a right angle with his left hand on the steering wheel and his right hand on the backrest of the passenger's seat. A few minutes later, we came to a railroad crossing where a train was rapidly approaching. Neil, wanting no part of having to wait at the crossing, gunned the engine to about 120. Large beads of sweat were dripping from my forehead down to my cheeks. With my heart in my throat, I made the sign of the cross as we went airborne flying across the tracks narrowly missing the train. Once I caught my breath and calmed my nerves, I said five Our Fathers and five Hail Marys, thanking God for guiding Neil and I through such a narrow escape.

When we arrived at the scene of the crash, we saw the tractor on the side of the road. One of its rear wheels had come off and was leaning against a tree and its spray unit had broken off the back. The driver, lying on top of the wreckage, was seriously injured. The vehicle that struck the tractor had swerved into a roadside ditch and was severely damaged. Its driver, however, received only minor injuries.

After we cleared the accident scene, I gave serious thought to asking Neil if I could walk back to the station to avoid any further reckless driving.

At 6 feet 4 inches tall, and 350 pounds with huge hands, Neil Ketchum was a physically imposing man. If an arrestee tried to take a swing at him, he would simply catch his fist in the air and throw him to the ground. Neil was also deeply religious. One thing he would not tolerate in his presence was cursing. For instance, a young male arrestee in the late 1960s called him a cocksucker. Neil told him to shut his mouth. The arrestee responded by telling him to fuck off. The officer proceeded to backhand him so hard that his body appeared to spin around three times before his shoes even moved.

"One Hell of a Crash"

Early August 1969

It was just before 7 P.M. when I entered the jail area to begin my Saturday night shift. I began to review some documents left behind by the previous deputies when Neil Ketchum, who happened to be the jailer that day, approached me from behind. "Well, let's go," he said.

"Where are we going?" I asked.

"You're the only one on patrol tonight," Neil replied. Suddenly, I remembered the son of our sheriff, Nick Check, got married earlier in the day and all the deputies were at the wedding reception. "It's just you and me kid," Neil said.

After gassing up the squad car and preparing for my shift, I heard Neil's voice come over the radio.

"374," he said, "we've got one hell of a crash with severe injuries near McDill Auto Wrecking."

I had never heard of the place. "Where the hell is *that?* I asked Neil.

"What? You don't know where McDill Auto Wrecking is?" he yelled, his deep, unmistakable voice reverberating over the radio.

Good thing I was alone since my face was flush with embarrassment.

"Just take Business 51 down to Double H and it's right there on the corner," Neil said. "The accident is at the intersection, get your ass moving!"

As I closed in on the south side of Stevens Point, the traffic on Business 51 near the accident scene had come to a standstill. Many drivers, seeing me approach, moved their vehicles against the guardrail. Gradually, I needled through them careful not to break off their mirrors. Driving across the bridge that spans McDill Pond I noticed in the water to my right the hood of a vehicle. With about 200 feet to go before reaching the intersection, I jumped out of my car and ran the rest of the way. Arriving via an accessible alternate route—Water Street to Whiting Avenue—Stevens Point Police Officer Jim Rogers met me at the scene.

It appeared that three people were heading out to dinner in a Chevy Impala: a seventy-two-year-old man, his seventy-one-year-old wife, and their thirty-six-year-old daughter. Due to the severe impact of the accident, father, mother, and daughter had been thrown through the driver's-side window of the Impala. Jim and I found the father lying face down in the middle of the intersection. A female bystander had stuffed her jacket under his face as he experienced convulsions that were causing his head to beat hard against the asphalt. Puddles of blood surrounded the man's body. He also had a huge hole on the right side his head, deep enough to where you could see into his skull; the result of striking metal debris on the road when he flew out of the car. About seventy-five feet away on the double yellow line was the man's wife lying unconscious with a faint pulse. Not far away was the man's daughter lying on her right side in a fetal position.

Ernie Groholski, an acquaintance of mine from Amherst, was traveling at about 40 miles per hour in his pickup truck. The Impala was doing about 15 or so since its driver, the father, had gunned the engine from a standstill at the intersection. Driving off Double H onto Business 51, the father needed to make a left-hand turn but he cheated the intersection and veered at an angle across the northbound lane to the southbound lane. Driving in the other direction was Ernie in his pickup. The ensuing collision occurred at a sharp angle where the truck struck the Impala between its left front tire and driver's-side door. The impact sucked the couple and their daughter out of the driver's-side window; pieces of their flesh and clothing attached to its perimeter confirming it. Other than the driver's side, every window in the Impala was intact. Even the windshield, though cracked from the inside, was still in one piece. But several indentations were evident from where the bodies made contact with the windshield before exiting through the driver's-side window.

Jim ran to his squad car to retrieve a huge stack of clean blankets, some of which were used to replace the bystander's blood-soaked jacket under the father's head so he wouldn't die from convulsions. Others were placed under the wife who was lying in the middle of the road. We were careful to keep her on her side so she wouldn't drown in her own blood. Jim, a long-time veteran of the Stevens Point police force, was known throughout the county as someone who couldn't stand the sight of blood. So he proceeded to stand back several feet from the scene with a flashlight in his hand and a look of grotesque on his face. The two ambulances he called had a difficult time making it through the traffic, which was now backed up for miles. But eventually they arrived and the father, miraculously alive at the time, was loaded into the first ambulance with his wife. The man was pronounced dead, however, at Saint Michael's. His wife was dead on arrival.

The impact of the accident was so great that it propelled the daughter, who was sitting in the backseat, out the driver's-side window like a cannonball over Ernie's truck. The woman's body proceeded to skid face down on the blacktop burning off her eyebrows and pulling the skin of her forehead down over her eyes. Her lips had been worn away and all of her front teeth were knocked out of her mouth. With her nose chiseled from her face and her breasts completely sheared off, her mangled body created a twenty-four-inch-wide stripe of human flesh that ran more than forty feet down the road. Shockingly, the woman had a slight pulse. Jim retrieved a case of bandages from the trunk of the squad car and we began to address her many wounds.

Given the potential for neck and back injuries, we didn't want to roll the woman onto her side. So we carefully applied bandages to her breast and facial and wounds while she lay face down. Gently, we rolled her onto a longboard and strapped her into a head and neck brace. She was then loaded into the second ambulance. Despite the gravity of her condition, the woman survived.

Pointing to Ernie, I turned to Jim and said, "That's the other driver. He's the one who hit them." Dressed in a white T-shirt and faded blue jeans, Ernie was covered head to toe with blood. But he didn't appear to have any serious injuries. When I approached him to ask some questions about how the accident unfolded, he answered me in slurred speech. At first, I thought perhaps Ernie had been drinking, but he was sober as a judge. The impact of the accident had caused the man to bite off two inches of his tongue. "Ernie, you've got to get to the hospital," I told him.

"I ain't ridin' wit no dead pipple," he said in a garbled manner pointing to the ambulance.

"Just get inside, Ernie," I countered. "There are no dead people."

"Tho me," he insisted. I opened the back the door to prove to him that there were no fatalities inside. The daughter was lying on her back with an oxygen mask on.

"Alwight," he said as he crawled into the ambulance.

With 10 P.M. approaching, the traffic on Business 51 had backed up in each direction for at least three miles. Southbound, in fact, was stuck all the way down to Plover. The people ensnared on the road had no chance of getting out. So at least one hundred of them had left their cars and surrounded the accident scene to get a closer look at what was going on. Several of those people asked me if they could be of any assistance. I answered that getting some of the automotive debris off the road would be a help so we could start alleviating the traffic congestion. Dressed in shirts and ties, a group of men hauled the engine from the Chevy Impala that was sitting in the middle of the road off to the side.

After more than two and a half hours of tending to injuries, cleaning up debris, taking photographs and measurements, and documenting every last detail of the chaotic accident, the scene was finally cleared.

Blinding Light Show

June 6, 1970

The excitement was building as I prepared for my first assignment to patrol. Traveling down County Trunk J during a severe thunderstorm, I had to strain my eyes to see the road in front of me. About thirty minutes into my shift, Mother Nature decided to put on a dazzling display of lightning. Suddenly, I received a radio call from dispatch.

"Headquarters to 374."

"Go ahead 374."

"We have a report of a lightning strike in Polonia. A house is on fire and the fire department has been dispatched."

"374 to headquarters, 10-4, I'm on my way."

Less than ten minutes later, I arrived at the scene to find the garage on fire and the flames were beginning to penetrate the house. The couple that lived there explained that they were sitting in the living room with their two children watching the weather forecast on television when they heard a loud crack and saw a flash of lightning. In a few seconds, the power failed. The man of the house said that when he went to the garage to check on the electrical panel he noticed flames on the roof. Thankfully, the family had evacuated and was standing outside in the street, albeit in a relentless downpour. The man, however, was making an ineffective attempt to salvage his fishing boat from the garage.

Seeing that he was struggling, I retrieved a long chain from the trunk of my squad car. Together we hooked one end to the boat and the other to the trailer hitch on the car and I was able to pull the vessel a safe distance from the house. Moments later, the fire department arrived and with help from the pouring rain, the flames soon were doused. Just then, I received another call from dispatch.

"Headquarters to 374."

"Go ahead headquarters."

"We have another fire caused by lightning," said the dispatcher. "This one is at the West River County Club. The man who called it in reported hearing multiple explosions, so you better hurry."

"10-4 dispatch. I'm on my way."

I explained to the family that I had another emergency to address telling them I would be back later to take the information I needed to complete my incident report. Soaking wet from the heavy rain, I jumped into my car and sped away.

The lightning was blinding as I drove to the club on the west side of Stevens Point. When I arrived, I found the fire department spraying water on the flames near the back of the building. More than fifty bottles of rum, tequila, gin, and bourbon whiskey had detonated like miniature bombs when the intense heat of the fire penetrated the liquor storage unit. Knowing there was a propane tank behind the unit, I feared the worst. But the fire chief wasted no time in assigning a truck and crew to pour water on the tank to keep it from exploding. With an assist from the rain, the fire was extinguished in less than thirty minutes.

I then drove back to Polonia to speak with the family and file my incident report.

Feelin' Groovy:
The Iola Rock Festival
June 26-28, 1970

At the beginning of my law enforcement career in the late 1960s my impression of hippies—ubiquitous as air at the time—was that they were lazy, long-haired, draft-dodging, irresponsible, Grateful Dead-following, pot-smoking individuals. But after dealing with them for a few years, I came to understand that they were friendly, peace-loving human beings, and, in many cases, well educated.

The early 1970s were simply an extension of the drug-crazed late 1960s. With young America still in revolt, you could see countless hippies walking around most any town in tie-dyed T-shirts giving the peace sign to each other with one hand while toking on a joint with the other. As the country remained entrenched in the Vietnam War, there were protests and riots. High school and college students were frustrated watching their friends come home to the states in body bags from a pointless war they didn't agree with. Drugs, sex, and, above all, music offered the perfect outlet for that frustration. Across America, young people sought to replicate the Woodstock experience of August 1969. And as the spring of 1970 approached, thousands of young Wisconsinites craved a collective outdoor music experience of their own.

A rock festival promoter approached a farmer in the town of New Hope about renting his vacant farm to promote outdoor music. Despite a great deal of negative feedback from residents in the area who opposed the idea, the deal was on.

Wisconsin's Woodstock, officially billed as the Sound Storm Festival, was held on a hillside farm owned by Irene York near Poynette in Columbia County, twenty-eight miles north of Madison. Taking place from April 24-26, 1970, more than 25,000 people attended. Most pitched tents on the fields and stayed for all three days. The crowd was incredible and the drugs flowed freely and openly. The festival was declared a success and it compelled others to try to organize a second one. They did, and it ended being up more like Altamont than Woodstock.

Concert Promoters International and Earth Enterprises bought a parcel of land that straddled the counties of Portage and Waupaca near the town of Iola, roughly sixty-five miles west of Green Bay. Their plan was to hold a "People's Fair," widely referred to as the Iola Rock Festival, to take place on the weekend of June 26-28, 1970. When the announcement of a new festival was made a week earlier officials of both counties talked about putting a halt to it for fear of criminal activity, but there was nothing they could do. At the time, Iola had no enforceable zoning laws.

The festival took place on a 200-acre partially wooded farm with a long inclined field that created a natural amphitheater. Advance tickets cost $10. A publicity poster for the event promised "Fresh Air! Nature! Music! Love! Fun! Water! Ponds and Streams!" while declaring "Street People, Come and Love!"

As part of the local law enforcement crew assigned to provide a police presence at the event, I prepared for the worst—drug use, intoxication, sex, theft, assault, injury, and crowd control. Officials of the two counties ordered us to stay out of the crowd and concentrate on maintaining security around the perimeter of the fairgrounds. Knowing that the festival would be overflowing with marijuana and other drugs, they took a somewhat lenient stance of its use and the myriad public nudity that often went along with it.

The only road into the fairgrounds backed up for more than eight miles delaying the rock festival's start. Bands that were supposed to start playing around noon on Friday didn't take the stage until after 6 P.M. But with the smell of marijuana wafting through the air, few seemed to mind.

By twilight, there were couples kissing with their arms wrapped around each other's waist listening to the music in the distance. Several girls wore an American flag as a sundress while many other girls walked around with their tops off for most of the weekend. There were countless longhaired friends of Jesus among a sea of tie-dye as far as the eye could see. There were also many oversized bongs in full view of law enforcement. In fact, the entire festival was one big outdoor drug market where attendees could buy any illegal substance they wanted. There was marijuana, hashish, cocaine, heroin, LSD, pretty much anything the kids could get their hands on. Many of the attendees hung paper plates from their tent openings that read "WEED" or "HASH" so others would know where to purchase their drugs of choice. The officers that worked the festival had no way to enforce drug laws since there were thousands of infractions. So the focus was on ensuring that the attendees didn't commit acts of violence or destroy property adjacent to the fairgrounds.

There was also a lot of alcohol at the festival. The grounds were littered with beer, wine, and whiskey bottles. Buzz-inducing substances, however, weren't the only problem facing law enforcement. Gratuitous nudity could be found at every turn and a number of couples had sex openly and often while large crowds cheered them on.

While working the checkpoint at the gate officers inspected vehicles for firearms and found quite a few which were confiscated. But some still made their way inside.

A Volkswagen microbus that had a dead deer tied to its roof pulled up to the gate. "What the hell are you doing with that deer?" I asked the driver of the vehicle.

"We found it on the side of the road," he replied. "Someone must have hit it."

"So what are you going to do with it?"

"We're going to eat it!" yelled one of the passengers. "This is our food for the entire weekend!"

Inside the fairgrounds, amenities were strained beyond capacity. There were only two telephones available for communication. The few toilets scattered about the property overflowed with human waste causing an insufferable stench that drew uncontrollable swarms of flies, gnats, and mosquitoes. With only twenty beds, the makeshift hospital tent was overwhelmed in trying to accommodate more than 3,500 medical emergencies.

The presence of outlaw bikers at the festival posed the biggest problem for law enforcement. A group of about thirty bikers from the Milwaukee area entered the festival illicitly by tearing down part of the fence toward the rear of the property. Heavily armed they felt they could do anything they pleased and take anything they wanted. On Saturday night, several of them climbed onto the stage while the Amboy Dukes (featuring a young Ted Nugent) were playing and began fighting with one of the security guards, eventually throwing him off the stage breaking several of his bones. The bikers went great lengths to intimidate the crowd with guns and switchblades openly displayed.

A tanker truck filled with water and surrounded by a chain link fence was one of the few sources of clean drinking water on the fairgrounds. But the fence didn't deter the bikers who knocked it down and took over the truck. They opened its top hatch and went swimming in the water. When they finished they urinated and defecated in it. Some of the festival attendees, unaware of what the bikers had done, drank some of the water from the truck.

My colleagues and I approached some of the bikers and asked them to leave. But with no uniformed police on the actual fairgrounds, there was no way to enforce their exit. The Portage County Sheriff's Department didn't have sufficient law enforcement authority to police anything at the festival beyond crowd and traffic control. As the bikers remained, reports of beatings, rapes, and robberies mounted during the overnight hours.

Tensions were on the rise.

At about 6:30 A.M. on Sunday, June 28, the last day of the festival, a large group of hippies got together and decided they had seen enough. They ascended a hill and began throwing bottles and rocks at the bikers that were camped just below. Others, armed with clubs and fence posts, attacked the bikers on foot. In response, the bikers climbed on their motorcycles and headed for the gate. As the throng of angry hippies pursued, the bikers' girlfriends sat with guns on the handlebars of the motorcycles shooting indiscriminately into the crowd wounding three attendees. Eventually, the hippies overwhelmed the bikers knocking them off their motorcycles. The bikers then fled on foot in fear for their lives, but not before watching the hippies stack their motorcycles in a pile and set them on fire. The bikers headed toward a flatbed truck that they used to flee. In an instant, three squad cars gave chase down the highway: the first driven by Deputy Robert Pallen, the second driven by me with Deputy Cliff Koziczkowski riding shotgun, and the third driven by Sergeant Doug Warner. As the first squad car crested a steep hill, Deputy Pallen locked the breaks after noticing the flatbed truck had stopped at the bottom of the hill. The bikers had formed a straight line across the road and were facing us armed with shotguns. When Pallen's squad car came to an abrupt stop, it gave me little time to react, causing me to skid toward it. Suddenly, the squad car behind me struck my car with such force that it pushed it on top of Pallen's car. Bumped and bruised after destroying three squad cars we somehow managed to crawl out of the wreck. Lying on the road at the top of the hill, we ordered the bikers to drop their weapons. Coming to their senses, the bikers surrendered with no shots fired. Handcuffed, they stayed at the scene until a bus arrived to transport them to the Portage County Jail. Although the bikers repeatedly called us "pigs" and "bacon" during the entire ordeal, they ultimately thanked us for saving their lives considering the beating they would've taken at the hands of the angry hippies.

About half of the bikers were arraigned on Monday morning, some of which were released on bond while others paid fines. Charges filed against the bikers included injury by reckless conduct, possession of concealed weapons, theft, rape, and attempted murder. Wounded attendees from Sunday's rumble were reported in good condition by Monday afternoon.

After the shootings, people started leaving the festival in droves. At its peak, we estimated the crowd to be at about 50,000. By Sunday evening, barely 5,000 people remained to see the last handful of bands.

The promoter of the Iola Rock Festival fled the state of Wisconsin and went into hiding never to be heard from again. In the weeks that followed a local ordinance was passed to limit or block similar events ensuring that a situation like this never occurred again in central Wisconsin. By February 1971, sixty-five of Wisconsin's seventy-two counties had adopted restrictions on mass gatherings. Subsequently, the brief era of the multiday rock festival began to fade.

Forty-five years later, the Iola Rock Festival remains a cultural benchmark in the history of central Wisconsin.

My Eyes Deceived Me
October 4, 1971

The U.S. Highway 51 bypass around Stevens Point was completed in early October 1971. It had been opened to traffic for only one day when Deputy Jim

Schultz and I were dispatched to an injury accident in the town of Dewey just north of Stevens Point.

Returning from dinner at a local restaurant, a four-door sedan pulled onto the new highway and was broadsided from the passenger's side at a high rate of speed. The accident pinned sixty-seven-year-old Kathy Harris* to the back seat of the vehicle.

Arriving at the scene, Jim and I feared that the woman might have neck and spinal injuries, so we cautiously pried open the left rear door. There was only room for one of us in the back seat to attend to her removal and first aid. On the floor between the seats, I checked Kathy's pulse. It seemed strong but she wasn't breathing and her face was starting to turn blue. I crawled into the back seat hoping to lift her up carefully from the floor. Jim crawled into the front seat to help stabilize her head while I lifted her. As I did, she began to slip from my arms due to the silky material of her dinner dress. Rather than allowing the woman to fall, I lunged forward to get a better grip on her body. The motion jolted her and with her head on my shoulder, she let out a gasp. Kathy began to cough, and then appeared to spit out her tongue. About two inches thick and eight inches long, it slid down the front of my shirt. As it turned out it, wasn't her tongue at all—she was choking on a massive blood clot that she coughed up when I shifted her body. We were able to pull her out of the car, place her on a stretcher, and get her into an awaiting ambulance. Then it was off to Saint Michael's.

Ironically, the fact that I almost dropped Kathy actually ended up saving her life. Until she regurgitated the blood clot, it had been stuck in her throat obstructing her ability to breathe.

Considering the severity of the accident the woman was fortunate to suffer only a few broken ribs.

Slippery When Wet

October 15, 1971

While patrolling on a rainy, gloomy night, I was dispatched to Old Wausau Road in the town of Hull to address a one-car accident with injuries. The involved vehicle, a Chevy convertible, had been traveling at a high rate of speed when it skidded broadside into a large oak tree. The impact was so severe that the car had wrapped perfectly around the tree. I was unable to locate the driver until I heard a faint moan. With the back seat folded in half, I could only see a person's fingertips sticking out, but I was relieved to know that the driver was still alive.

Surveying the situation, I tried to figure out how to pull the man safely from the car. I called for a towing service and suggested that they send two trucks. When they arrived, I conferred with the owner, Tommy Schultz, as to how we could pry the car from the tree without killing the driver. We decided to anchor a truck to one side of the car while the other truck proceeded to unwrap it from the tree. The process of pulling the car in both directions took thirty minutes. After nearly tearing the car in half, we finally created an opening in the middle allowing me to pull the driver out. Shining my flashlight on the man, I could see that the right side of his skull looked as though a hatchet had swung through it. The bark of the oak tree had formed deep gouges in the man's face, deep enough to see through his cheeks, and his right eye was hanging from its socket. I couldn't believe the man had a pulse. After I wrapped his face and skull, he was transported to Saint Michael's by ambulance.

I took skid mark measurements and photos, and then cleared the scene. Shortly after, I drove to the hospital to get the man's personal identification and check on his condition only to find that he had died. When I retrieved his driver's license from his wallet, I was shocked to learn that the driver was John Wojtasiak, a second cousin of mine! The accident had mutilated his face to the point where I didn't even recognize him.

The hardest part of the job came next: notifying the family of the tragedy, a task made more difficult considering it involved one my own relatives.

Later that evening I arrived at the home of John's parents and rang the doorbell. His mother came to the door. Seeing a sad look in my eyes she sensed that something tragic had happened. When I conveyed the news of her son's death, she nearly fell to the floor.

"Oh, my God!" she said. "Did he suffer?"

"No, I don't believe he did," I replied.

With tears in their eyes, John's parents joined the coroner and drove to the morgue to identify their son.

Accident or Arson?

October 23, 1971

Early in my shift, I was dispatched to a house fire in the town of Biron about twelve miles west of Plover. The home, located on Biron Drive overlooking the Wisconsin River, was built in such a fashion that it had long steel beams reaching out over the river.

The man who owned the home, fifty-year-old bachelor Peter Wilkins,* apparently had a few dollars in the bank. He was known around town as a ladies' man for the many female guests he would often entertain, but he happened to be alone at the time of the blaze.

Though the fire department was already tending to Peter's home, it was still engulfed in flames when I arrived with a fellow deputy. The top floor of the home had collapsed to the bottom floor and there was nothing more than a pile of smoldering embers at its center. After the embers cooled to a point where we could walk on them, we noticed the sizzling trunk of a human body in what used to be the home's living room. The legs of the trunk were burnt to a crisp while part of an arm was entangled in the frame of a metal chair. The skull had exploded, likely from the intense heat. Wafting in the air was the horrific smell of burned flesh.

It appeared that Peter passed out after grabbing the metal chair and perished moments later. Attempting to retrieve his fire extinguisher in the kitchen the man was overtaken by heat and smoke. He then burned through the living room floor falling straight down to the bottom of the house.

The first order of business was to remove Peter's bodily remains from the burnt home. We retrieved a rubber body bag from the trunk of our squad car and then used flat shovels to lift what was left of the man's body and place it inside. Attempting to carry the bag outside, we took three steps before the still-boiling remains melted right through it. We let things cool for a while and then placed the remains into another bag where they were held successfully.

Difficult as it was an autopsy was performed on Peter's charred body. All that remained were parts of the rib cage, spine, and pelvis, but there were no indications of any intrusions from weapons of any sort and no bones were crushed from severe impact. The investigation revealed that the fire was accidental, perhaps due to smoking or a fireplace that may have overheated and spread into the house.

Suicide Scare

November 15, 1971

The biggest learning experience of my nineteen-year law enforcement career was how to deal with people effectively. But simply talking to them at their level was sometimes hard to do. One of the greatest tests for an officer is talking a person down when they are threatening suicide. Care must be taken not to trigger a situation, keeping it as calm as possible.

On this chilly autumn day, I was dispatched to address Mike Hardek,* a local man staying at a boarding house. Mike was threatening to shoot himself with a deer rifle. Since Sergeant Kingsley Fletcher knew the man, a notorious drunk, he decided to accompany me even though the call was in Stevens Point. When we arrived at the house, Mrs. Meshak, its owner, met us at the door saying that Mike was in a room at the top of the staircase. We went up the stairs to find the door open and the room dark. As I peered in, the glow of a dimly lit street lamp allowed me to see the silhouette of a man sitting on a chair next to a window. Sure enough, it was Mike Hardek holding a .30-30 Winchester rifle with the end of the barrel tucked snugly under his chin pointing upward. Sergeant Fletcher talked to the man, who appeared inebriated, to keep him distracted so he wouldn't blow his head off. Mike then looked at me and asked who I was. I identified myself and asked him what was so terrible to consider something like this. I nearly soiled my pants when he turned the rifle in my direction, three feet from my chest with its hammer cocked. "You wanna go with me, deputy?" Mike asked with a sneer. With shaking hands, the man held the rifle in that position for what seemed like an eternity. But the last thing I wanted to do was reach for my gun. After all, I was there to prevent a suicide. How would I justify shooting the man in self-defense? "Just give me the rifle, son," Sergeant Fletcher said a few minutes later, "and we'll forget this ever happened."

With the weapon still pointed at my chest Mike began to think for a moment, unsure of what to do. He then stared me in the eye with a wicked grin. Convinced that the man was about to shoot me I started saying my prayers. But in a matter of seconds, Mike's grin turned to a smile and he pulled the rifle back. He then handed it to Sergeant Fletcher. I took a deep breath, grateful the ordeal was over.

We took Mike to the station, but instead of jailing him, we contacted county health officials to ensure that the man received proper psychiatric care.

Fear notwithstanding, being shot to death while trying to prevent a suicide would have been a disconcerting way for a law enforcement officer to die.

Nevertheless, if you could locate the undershorts I wore that night, you would probably find racing stripes within.

Monsters in the Attic

December 9, 1971

A call from the Village of Park Ridge in Portage County stated that a local woman, sixty-two-year-old Hattie Banka,* was found dead at her home.

The sheriff's department had been summoned to Hattie's property several times before as she reported hearing "strange noises." When Deputy Ray Spielman checked out her property just a few weeks before, she told him there were "monsters running around in the attic" and they were keeping her up at night.

At the time of the deputy's arrival, Hattie happened to be making a pot of coffee. "Would you like a cup of joe?" she asked.

Ray, thinking it would be impolite to decline, answered, "Sure, I'd love a cup."

The coffee, fresh out of the pot, was boiling hot. The deputy took one sip and nearly burned his top lip. Hattie then poured herself a cup. She raised it to her lips and without so much as a flinch downed the scorching liquid in a matter of seconds as if it were a cool glass of water on a warm summer day.

Something is seriously wrong with this lady, Ray thought.

"There are definitely monsters up there in the attic," Hattie told the deputy as she wiped a stray drop of coffee from her mouth.

Just then, the wind began to blow, and a sound emerged from the direction of the attic—tap, tap, tap…

When Ray went outside to investigate the noise, he discovered that the wide flat wire running up the side of the house to the television antennae was flapping in the wind and banging against the roof outside the attic. He went back inside the house and explained to Hattie what it was.

"No, no, no," she said emphatically. "I know there are monsters living up there."

The deputy assured Hattie that he looked at the top of the house near the attic and that everything was fine but she refused to believe him. He then returned to the office to write a report on the incident documenting that the woman possessed "strange tendencies."

When I arrived at Hattie's house to answer the current call, night had fallen and the property was dark throughout. I got out of the car with a flashlight, walked up to the porch, and rang the doorbell. There was no answer. I tried the doorknob but it was locked. I walked around the outside of the house to try to shine some light into the windows but all the curtains were drawn. As I approached the garage, I noticed the service door was closed, but not locked. So I stepped inside with my flashlight and spotted a white Chevy Impala with what appeared to be blood splattered on its passenger's-side door. Moving in closer, I saw the feet of a human being lying on the garage floor protruding just beyond a wooden rail. Thinking there might be a murderer on the property, I drew my gun. A young deputy at the time, I wasn't sure whether I should continue to investigate the scene, wait for backup to arrive, or go back to the squad car and summon the SWAT team. Curiosity getting the best of me, I decided to investigate.

Walking closer to the door leading from the house to the garage, I spotted the body of Hattie Banka lying face up in a substantial pool of blood. There was a bullet wound on her forehead between her eyes. I stood over the body with my camera to get a close-up picture of the wound. With no way to hold the flashlight on target, I held it in my mouth freeing both hands to operate the camera. Just as I was about to snap a picture the neighbor who reported the grisly discovery returned to the scene. Without making a sound, she put her hand on my shoulder. Startled, I jumped up and nearly swallowed my flashlight. "Holy shit, don't ever do that again!" I hollered thankful that I didn't have a gun in my hand.

The neighbor said she didn't want to return to the scene until she saw a squad car. Through tearful eyes, she said that she and Hattie were good friends and they would check on each other's welfare nearly every day. She claimed that her friend had been acting strange lately and often spoke of hearing noises in her home. She also said Hattie was going to take a vacation, but not before killing the monsters in her attic. Affirming the woman's statement was a set of luggage leaning against the wall of the garage, packed and ready to go.

Returning to my squad car I called the coroner since a death had occurred. I also wanted to summon Sergeant Fletcher to the scene. Several minutes later, both men arrived concurrently.

The first thing the coroner wanted to do was determine the time of death. So he picked up Hattie's right arm to check for rigor mortis. When he did, I saw the butt of a pistol protruding from under the woman's back. Since the weapon was covered in blood, I put my pencil through the trigger guard to pull it away from the body, which was lying about six feet from a folding ladder. When I looked up, I saw a drop panel slightly opened over the ceiling of the garage. Considering the woman's luggage, I began to figure out what happened. After likely hearing noises again, she retrieved the pistol from her house where her late husband had kept it, determined to get rid of those "monsters" once and for all.

I surmised that Hattie was on the ladder with pistol at the ready. To get into the attic she needed to climb up and then hoist herself through the drop panel. But she lost her balance and accidentally pulled the trigger on the gun firing a bullet into her head behind her right ear. The bullet exited through her forehead between the eyes. The woman then fell off the ladder landing on her back. The blood on the side of the Chevy Impala had splashed from the exit wound. After examining the woman, the coroner said the bullet probably spun around inside her head several times before it departed.

Deputy Pete Thrun, working the same shift with me that night, helped me remove Hattie's body and lock up the house. We then drove back to the office to write our reports since Sergeant Fletcher wanted all of our paperwork finished before retiring for the evening.

With a cup of coffee in his hand, the sergeant walked down the hallway to where Pete and I were typing at our desks. Considering that I was a newbie, he stood next to me every few minutes to make sure I was completing the paperwork correctly. "You have quite a bit done already," he said as he glanced over my shoulder. "And it's a good thing you took those pictures. We'll get them developed tomorrow. How about some fingerprints? You did you get them, right?

"Um, no sir, we didn't."

Thick veins protruded from Sergeant Fletcher's neck. I could tell he was furious. "Well, Hattie's body is at Rusin Funeral Home,* so you better haul your ass over there and get them! We have the gun, and there are prints on the gun. We need that woman's prints!"

After ordering Pete to accompany me, the sergeant handed us the print kit complete with blotter and ink and my partner and I were on our way.

We rang the funeral home doorbell but got no answer. The door was unlocked so I opened it and walked to the office area but there was no one there. I saw lights on and heard loud rock and roll music playing in the basement at the bottom of the stairway. At the top of the stairs, I tapped my flashlight along the rail to announce my presence. Finally, Ned Rusin,* the undertaker and owner of the funeral home, heard me. "Hi there," he said, "come on down!" Pete and I entered the basement and saw Hattie's body lying in a metal tray where Ned was washing it in preparation for the embalming. The woman's hands were clasped together on her chest and her head was resting on a block as he ran icy cold water on the body to increase its stiffness. "What are you guys doing here?" the undertaker asked. "Is there something I can help you with?"

"No, we just need to get fingerprints from this deceased woman," I answered.

"Be my guest, sirs," Ned said. "But good luck, her fingers are pretty damn stiff!"

Indeed, in our effort to bend the woman's fingers away from each other to roll them on the block, we accidentally broke some of them due to their rigor.

Meanwhile, the undertaker was preparing to do the embalming. As we all stood next to the body, he glanced at the hole in the woman's forehead and then looked toward me.

"Is that a bullet wound?" he asked.

"Yes, it is," I replied.

"That's really strange how it exited her head like that."

Leaning over the body to get the prints without further damage, I didn't realize that Ned had stuck a cleaning rod into the woman's head. Protruding out of the exit wound on the woman's forehead it was pointing right in my face with a piece of brain hanging on the end of it. It took a deep breath and a long step backward to keep me from vomiting on the corpse. Seeing my repellent expression the undertaker laughed his ass off as he played air guitar to his rock and roll music.

After a full hour of failed attempts, Pete and I finally got the fingerprints we needed. We then returned to the office, finished our reports, and drove home.

When I climbed into bed that night I could still see Hattie's face staring at me, brains and all.

Footprints in the Snow

January 18, 1972

On one of the chilliest days in Wisconsin history, the temperature outside had plunged to roughly fifty degrees below zero. But that didn't stop Buena Vista resident Herbert Zychowski* from wandering out into the cold. After sipping hot chocolate by a cozy fire in his farmhouse, the seventy-six-year-old man, who suffered from dementia, walked out his back door and into the frigid Wisconsin countryside. Carefully, Herbert ambled along a lengthy hedgerow for about a quarter mile through the accumulated snow. While doing so, he would take a few steps, stop briefly to rest, and then shed an article of his clothing, which he left lying on the wintry landscape. First, it was his mittens, then his knit cap. After a few more steps, he shed his flannel shirt. Then, he took off his boots, socks, trousers, long johns, and underwear. Completely naked, Herbert lay down in the snow to take a nap.

After following the man's trail of footprints—some made by boots, others by bare feet—I found him lying peacefully, stiff as a board, dead from hypothermia.

Kidney Transplant

February 20, 1972

While working the nightshift as a jailer and dispatcher I received a call from Saint Michael's regarding a patient awaiting a kidney donor. In critical condition and no longer responding to dialysis, the man's kidneys were failing fast. The University of Wisconsin Hospital in Madison had a matching kidney taken from an auto accident fatality. The problem was that there was a two-hour time frame to get the man to Madison.

With Sheriff Nick Check out of town on vacation, I called Captain Bill Kvatek at his home since he wanted to be made aware of all emergencies. I explained the situation and asked him what he wanted to do about the transport. I presumed that Bill was going to make the run since he told me to have a squad car gassed up and ready to go upon his arrival. Minutes later the captain stepped off the elevator at the station wearing jeans and a T-shirt with sleep still in his eyes. "You got the car gassed up?" he asked.

"Yes I do, Captain!" I answered.

"Okay, I'll take the helm here at dispatch," he said, "You have only two hours to get there. Be on your way!"

A bit surprised that Bill gave me the job I hurried to Saint Michael's. The nuns that worked there introduced me to Ben Antoniewicz,* the kidney patient. I shook his hand and then led him out to the squad car. After safely securing him in his seat belt, I wasted no time in heading for Madison about 95 miles south. Seeing that Ben's skin was beginning to lose its normal tone, I zipped away from the hospital parking lot knowing that time was of the essence.

Merging onto U.S. Highway 51, I put the pedal to the metal. In the midst of a ruthless winter, the snowdrifts along the highway were ten to twelve feet tall. But the road itself was dry and clear allowing me to fly along at 135 mile per hour for most of the transport. About half way down the highway, I saw flashing blue and red lights reflecting off the snow. It appeared that a squad car had picked me up on its radar. Speeding by him, I watched the car disappear in the rear view mirror as he gave chase not even coming close to catching me.

When we arrived at Exit 151 for Madison, we began to see the lights of the state Capitol building. Thankfully, University Hospital was located right behind it. Ben never uttered a single word from the time we left Saint Michael's until the time we got to Madison. I drove up to the hospital door where a nurse and four orderlies came out to the squad car and loaded the man on a gurney. As they did, I walked inside to the front desk and asked the receptionist if I could use the telephone. After receiving permission, I called Bill.

"Captain, I'm here at the hospital," I informed him.

"What do you mean you're at the hospital?" he squawked. "You have two hours to drive to Madison. Now get your ass going!"

"But Captain, I'm trying to tell you that I'm already here in Madison."

Bill was in shock, and perhaps in awe, that I had driven there so quickly.

"You crazy bastard!" he yelled. "Are you freakin' nuts?"

From the time I got the call from Saint Michael's to my arrival at University Hospital in Madison, a total of one hour and forty minutes had lapsed. If we could locate the squad car in a junk yard today, you would probably see the deep fingernail gouges on the dashboard left by the kidney patient. At twenty-five-years old, I was still at an age where high-speed runs were fun and exciting.

Later, I learned that the kidney transplant performed on Ben was successful and the man was able to lead a normal life.

Before Susan Smith and
Andrea Yates There Was...

March and November 1972

On the frosty morning of March 14, 1972, I stopped at a local convenience store for a hot cup of coffee to start my morning. Before I was able to take a sip a call came over the radio from dispatch that a vehicle had been found partially submerged in the Wisconsin River.

It appeared that twenty-eight-year-old Elizabeth Berna, a mother of three children from Wisconsin Rapids, veered off the oak and birch-lined River Road on the southern fringe of Stevens Point and onto an ice sheet covering the river. Elizabeth purportedly pulled her three children out of the vehicle before it began to sink. Two of them escaped an icy fate, but a third child, fifteen-month-old Bruce, drowned. Elizabeth told authorities that while rescuing her five-year-old son Brian and three-year-old daughter Michelle, her younger son fell from her arms and into the dark, frigid waters.

Captain Bill Kvatek, Deputy Stan Potocki, and I went out with our boat to try to drag the river for the boy's body but were unsuccessful. As it turned out, the current had pushed the body against a submerged tree stump roughly 175 feet downstream, which is where I ended up retrieving it with an eight-foot dredging pole. The boy's body, dressed in a solid blue snowsuit, was in the fetal position when I pulled it out of the water. With tears in my eyes, I wrapped the body tightly in a blanket and placed it gently in the backseat of our Ford Bronco. I then drove back to the office and waited for Bill and Stan to return from the scene.

Local law enforcement documented the incident as an accident. But several officials viewed it with skepticism believing that Elizabeth intended to kill herself and, perhaps, all of her children. Whether Brian and Michelle witnessed their mother drop the boy into the river remains unclear.

Soon after Bruce's death, Elizabeth Berna, whom some neighbors considered erratic, nervous, and high-strung, underwent psychiatric treatment. Upon completion several months later, she was released to the custody of her husband, Robert.

Nearly eight months later on the Monday morning of November 13, another car driven by Elizabeth plunged into the Wisconsin River. This time, the mother and her two children were drowned.

Local law enforcement considered the mishap suspicious since it occurred at the exact same location and almost the same hour as the first incident. In addition, all three individuals were wearing much of the same clothing that was worn during the first incident.

Elizabeth's husband, Robert, told police that he last saw his wife and children at about 6 A.M. on Monday morning when she made breakfast for him. Robert claimed that before he went to work his wife told him she planned to spend most of the day sewing. He also said that Elizabeth had suffered from depression since the loss of their son Bruce.

Three hours after breakfast, Elizabeth's car left the road within five feet of the point where it veered off in March. It then traveled out about fifteen feet from the river's banks onto the ice where it sank in roughly ten feet of water. At 1:10 P.M., a passing motorist saw the roof of the car as it was visible under the clear water. There was no indication that Elizabeth's vehicle had skidded or attempted to brake. The woman chose the same spot to drive off the road since the guardrail was low offering the best chance for a vehicle to crash through it.

Portage County Coroner Emil Przekurat said that similar circumstances, including the location of both incidents, the absence of skid marks, and Elizabeth's apparent state of mind, suggested that the drowning was intentional. The body of daughter Michelle was found lodged under the passenger seat of the vehicle while son Brian was in the backseat fastened tightly with a seatbelt. The coroner also inferred that Michelle might have been strangled with a belt, perhaps in the vehicle or at home, before she drowned.

(In helping to retrieve Elizabeth Berna's vehicle from the river, Sergeant Mark Hemmrich descended into the icy water and hooked a cable for Tommy Schultz's wrecking service. While doing so, he slipped on a submerged rock and wrenched his back. A resilient man, Mark continued to work while receiving treatment for his injury.)

✳ ✳ ✳

The Berna family drownings shed a nationwide spotlight on the release of psychiatric patients before conceivably being ready. The consensus of the central Wisconsin community was that Elizabeth Berna, already a suspect in the killing of her youngest child, was released back into society only to kill herself and her remaining two children.

Fatal Auto Accident
and a Shocking Reaction
October 4, 1972

At about 2 A.M. I was dispatched to an auto accident with serious injuries. Deputy Gerald Thrun and I arrived at the scene simultaneously to observe twenty-seven-year-old Jennifer Ross* pinned behind the wheel of her four-door sedan. The vehicle had struck a pickup truck, which suffered extensive front-end damage. The driver of the truck, a thirty-year-old man, was standing by his vehicle with minor facial lacerations. The sedan rested at an angle in the middle of Jordan Road, the result of a head-on collision. According to witnesses, the driver of the pick-up truck wasn't speeding, but Jennifer *was*, likely in a hurry to get home to her husband and children after being out so late. She was returning from Jordan Park, a quiet county recreational area where illicit liaisons often went down after dark.

Jennifer, wearing dark blue jeans and a denim jacket, was struggling to breathe. I looked down and noticed blood dripping from the bottom of the door onto the blacktop. In a soft, fading voice, the woman begged us to get her out of the car.

Gerald and I theorized that the best way to accomplish this without causing more bodily damage was to remove the seat. Thankfully, we carried a tool kit in the trunk of the squad car. Gerald retrieved a socket wrench, pried the rear door open, and crawled into the back seat, removing the bolts that held the seat track. He pulled the seat back slowly while I slid my hands behind the woman's back. Holding her in place with wool blankets to avoid further injury, I could see that the woman's ribs were broken and protruding out of her back. They had slashed through her jacket like the edges of razor-sharp knives. "Gerry, it's really bad," I said.

"What do you want me to do?" he asked.

"Slowly, I want you to pull the seat back a little more."

When he did, Jennifer let out a subdued but painful-sounding moan. She then took a few shallow breaths, closed her eyes, and died in my arms.

As we removed the woman's body from the vehicle, we could see that the impact of the accident had driven the lower half of her spine downward out of her back and through her posterior, protruding through the seat of her blue jeans.

Minutes later, an ambulance arrived to transport the body to the hospital. The toxicology report on both drivers involved in the accident indicated that alcohol or drugs were not a factor.

Gerald and I finished clearing the scene at about 3 A.M. and then drove back to the office. As Sergeant Doug Warner was just leaving to go home for the night he offered to accompany me to the residence where Jennifer lived in the Village of Whiting to inform her next of kin of the accident; in this case, her husband, Josh,* who was at home caring for two small children.

Standing on the porch with our hats in our hands, Doug and I knocked a few times and Jennifer's husband came to the door. Seeing two law enforcement officers at his doorstep, the man's facial expression was hardly one of sadness or surprise.

"So what happened?" Josh inquired.

I asked the man if we could enter his house. "Sure, come in and have a seat," he said. He then looked at Doug and me with a steely gaze. "So where the hell was she?"

"Sir, your wife was involved in an accident near Jordan Park," I replied. "Unfortunately, she didn't survive."

"Well, the bitch finally got hers," he said with a smirk on his face. "At long last that fucking slut got what was coming to her. Here I am at home with our two young boys and she's out whoring around. Serves her right."

Doug and I looked at each other in shock.

"Is that all you have for me, gentlemen?" Josh inquired as he led us to the door.

"Yes, sir," I answered.

"Then I'll bid you farewell," he said. "Have a good night."

Don't Take Things So Literally
October 10, 1972

The sheriff's department dispatcher received an emergency call from a woman who claimed that her father-in-law had suffered a heart attack. He had apparently fallen to the ground, pulseless.

"Is the man breathing?" asked the dispatcher.

"No," replied the woman.

The dispatcher told the woman to stay on the line while he sent out an ambulance. Explaining it would be fifteen minutes until arrival he told the woman she would have to start performing CPR.

"I have no idea what CPR is," she stated.

"That's okay," the dispatcher said. "I'll walk you through it."

"Alright," the woman said with a loud exhale, "let's give it a try."

"First clear the airway," he said, "then pinch the nose shut, and apply mouth to mouth. We need to get air to the man's lungs to keep his brain alive."

The woman claimed that her father-in-law's tongue was blocking air from getting to his lungs.

"You need to pinch the nose with one hand and pin the tongue down with the other," the dispatcher instructed.

"Okay, I got it," said the woman. "I think it's actually working. His chest is expanding with each breath."

The ambulance arrived a short time later and an emergency worker took over CPR during transport to Saint Michael's.

Later, when I spoke with the ambulance operator, he asked who the dispatcher was that guided the woman through the administration of CPR. "I'm not sure," I answered. "Why do you ask?"

"When I arrived at the house I found the victim lying on his back," he said, "and his tongue was fastened to his bottom lip with a large safety pin."

I could only shake my head in response. The victim died on arrival to the hospital.

Don't Swerve to Avoid Deer

October 27, 1972

During the late afternoon Arnold Pankiewicz* drove his black Ford LTD into Stevens Point via County Trunk C at about eighty mile per hour. As he sped past the vehicle in front of him, its driver saw a line of deer cross the road from a marsh on the right heading into the woods on the left. Suddenly, the driver witnessed Arnold's brake lights, and in a split second, there was nothing but a cloud of smoke. Because he was traveling at such a high rate of speed, it appeared that Arnold didn't see the deer until it was too late. The fifty-five-year-old man locked his brakes and swerved to the left in an attempt to avoid a collision. He then veered to the right to try to stay on the road; otherwise, his Ford would have ended up in the woods. When he did, it caused the LTD to flip several times on its side. According to the witness, the vehicle then turned on its grill and flipped tail over nose three times before sliding about

150 feet. The final flip ejected Arnold through the driver's-side window and the vehicle landed on its roof pinning the man facedown underneath as it skidded. The impact created a yellowish smear of blood and guts on the asphalt that changed to a peculiar-looking blueish gray and then a shade of orange up to where the LTD was resting.

When the wrecker arrived to lift the vehicle, some of Arnold's body was attached to its roof while the rest of it was still smeared on the coarse asphalt of County Trunk C. None of the man's body parts could be positively identified, since the 2,000-pound pressure of the LTD on top of him had compressed his bodily remains to the width of a pancake.

Just as I retrieved a shovel and push broom from the trunk of my squad car, the local fire department arrived with its tanker. I broke loose Arnold's bodily remains from the road so the tanker could wash them away. In addition, I was able to scrape about fifteen pounds of Arnold's remains from the roof of his vehicle into a body bag. This way I had something to present to the undertaker as opposed to leaving a dead body on the highway.

Raging Bull

October 29, 1972

On a cool, crisp late Sunday afternoon, the sheriff's dispatcher received an injury call from a farm near Junction City just west of Stevens Point. Arriving at the scene, I spoke to a woman who told me that her father, Virgil,* was leading a Holstein bull out of the barn with a rope when he became tangled and was dragged to a swamp. I radioed in and informed the dispatcher that I would be in pursuit on foot.

I ran to my squad car and took my 12-gauge shotgun from the gunlock. I then began following the drag marks in the dirt. They had crossed a recently harvested cornfield where only ten-inch-high stalk stubble remained. There was a great deal of blood on the stubble indicating that Virgil's body had been pierced by the razor-sharp ends. I could see that the drag marks extended across the field to a barbed wire fence adjacent to a forest. The 1,600-pound bull had stampeded through the fence as if it were made of tissue paper.

As darkness slowly crept, I took out my flashlight and began scanning the area ahead of me, the crunch of gravel under my feet the only discernable noise. After walking a few yards, I noticed the bull standing right in front of me. With his head down, he was clearly tired from dragging the farmer for such a long distance. The bull was positioned behind a one-foot high bump of dirt along the fence line. As I carefully inched toward him, he snorted and raised his head exposing Virgil's body tied tightly to it by the rope. I moved closer toward the bull to get a clean shot at its head without hitting the farmer being careful since I was shooting 00 buckshot, which spreads a pattern of large pellets. The bull snorted wildly as I trained the light in his eyes. About six feet away, I fired a shot that struck him between the eyes knocking him down. Even though the animal suffered a split skull, it surprisingly began to kick and then rolled over onto Virgil's body. At once, I jumped the fence, stuck my .357 magnum into his ear, and fired. There was no more movement.

Virgil's trampled body had been gashed wide open. The man likely died before the bull ever stopped dragging him through the corn stubble. I placed the physical remains into a body bag and loaded them into an awaiting ambulance.

When I went inside the farmer's house to discuss his death with his family, I learned a shocking fact: His father also died after being trampled by a bull—on the same farm, forty years ago to the day, October 29, 1932.

Hintz Commits Suicide?

November 18, 1972

Claude* and Martha* Hintz (no relation to me), a husband and wife in the town of Sharon, were experiencing marital problems. Claude, apparently fed up with his marriage and, perhaps, life in general, had threatened suicide several times over recent months and this day would prove no different. When I arrived at the house, the man was mumbling incessantly about the problems he was having with his wife whom he called a "useless bitch" at least a dozen times. The couple was in the midst of yet another argument and Claude, holding a high-powered .30-06 rifle in his hand, was threatening to kill himself. Martha, however, didn't believe him since he had made such threats before. "You don't have the fuckin' guts to kill yourself," she declared. "Is that so?" Claude countered with a smartass smile on his face. He placed the rifle against his abdominal and fired. The blast propelled the man's liver from his body across the living room where it came to a rest under the coffee table. But he was still alive. Martha, shocked that her husband called her bluff, hurried to the telephone to call an ambulance.

Claude Hintz sat on the living room floor against the wall with a gaping hole in his stomach. As he talked about how bad his life was, and how his wife would constantly harass him, I couldn't help but glance over at his liver lying on the rug. Suddenly, I heard the ambulance approaching in the distance, but it was all for naught. Claude died moments later, but only after calling his wife a useless bitch one final time.

Careful with that Coat!

December 18, 1972

Depression may not be the first thing a person thinks about in relation to a terminal cancer diagnosis considering the most common notions that come to mind are fear, despair, and a sense of urgency. But depression can play a significant role in how well a cancer patient fares. Although there are millions of cancer survivors in the United States today, there are, unfortunately, those who will eventually succumb to their disease. And some of those people refuse to wait for a less-than-desirable end to their lives.

Such was the case with sixty-five-year-old Portage County resident Max Olsen.* A lifelong bachelor, Max lived on a farm that he owned with his younger brother. Depressed after being diagnosed with terminal cancer, the man decided that he didn't want to live with the enduring pain so he took his own life.

Max carried a .410 shotgun into the bathroom, placed the weapon to his right temple, and pulled the trigger. A .410 fires a small round but the impact of the shot sucked the man's face into his head and compressed the size of his skull to only about three inches thick. Bits of brain, hair, and skin were splattered on most everything behind where Max was standing. A good portion of the man's brain, however, had blown into the kitchen where it lay in the middle of the floor. The rest of it had splashed all the way up the doorframe that separated the bathroom from the kitchen.

While inspecting the scene Coroner Joe Bodzislaw walked from the kitchen into the bathroom wearing a sleek black top coat unaware that Max's brains were dripping only inches away. Throwing me a quizzical look, Joe inquired, "What do you think of this situation?"

"Be careful, Joe, don't lean back!" I yelled seeing his close proximity to the bespattered mess. But it was too late.

"Why? What's going on?" he asked.

The dead man's brains, in colors of yellow and orange, were dripping down the back of the coroner's coat. "Joe, please pull your coat off—carefully."

He did, and then looked at the back of it. "What the hell is all this gooey crap?"

"It's part of Max Olsen's brain, Joe! That's what I've been trying to tell you!"

Casually, the coroner used his bare hands to wipe some of the brains off the back of his coat and then wrung them out adding to the mess on the kitchen floor.

"It's no big deal," Joe said with a smile. "I'll have my wife wash off the rest of it when I get home."

I couldn't help but feel sorry for Mrs. Bodislaw having to clean up after Joe and his messy job.

Moments later, an ambulance arrived to transport Max's body to the morgue at Saint Michael's.

Night of the Green Flies

February 10, 1973

Even though I loved working in law enforcement, there were several occupational situations that I dreaded. Such as when a mail carrier would notify the sheriff's office to say that letters and newspapers were beginning to pile up outside someone's home.

On a bitter winter's evening, a carrier in Stevens Point found it suspicious that Gibson Janosik,* an eighty-three-year-old man that lived on his regular route wasn't retrieving the mail from his mailbox. When he walked up to his porch and knocked on the door, he noticed a reeking smell coming from the house. Immediately, he called the sheriff's department to have someone come out and check on things.

Together, Joe Bodzislaw and I reported to the address. We opened the door to discover Gibson lying on his back. A lifelong bachelor, the octogenarian appeared to have died of natural causes while resting comfortably on his couch.

Joe grabbed the elderly man's feet as I attempted to grab his shoulders so we could drag him into a body bag and put him on a stretcher for transport. We had moved the body only a few inches when its flesh started to crack and hundreds of maggots began to crawl out of it. When I finally got a firm grip under Gibson's shoulders to pick him up off the couch, a noxious gas emanated from the man's mouth. It was hot inside the house seeing as the heat had been turned up due to the bitter cold weather outside. That only helped make the gas inside the man that much fouler. Making matters worse, a swarm of bright green flies began to flutter out of Gibson's mouth and nose swiftly making their way up my arms and onto my face. The man's decaying body was at the mercy of the countless maggots that had been laying eggs inside of it. "Dan, have you ever seen anything like this before?" the coroner asked.

"No I haven't," I replied, "and I never want to see it again."

As I swatted the seemingly endless stream of flies from my face, Joe got quite a chuckle out of it.

Nonetheless, the ordeal turned my stomach to where it was hard for me eat for several days.

Next Time, Come Home Sober
May 17, 1973

A domestic dispute was called into dispatch from Saint Michael's Hospital. When officers arrived there, they found a man receiving treatment for serious head injuries.

During the course of the investigation, it was learned that David Sherwood* had stopped after work at a local tavern in the town of Stockton. After staying longer and drinking much more than he should have, the man went home inebriated. His wife, angry at the late hour of her husband's arrival, yelled at him when he walked through the front door and continued as he sat at the kitchen table to eat his dinner. Tired of his wife's shouting, the man slapped her across the face after he finished his meal. In response, she grabbed a cast iron skillet and, standing on her tippy toes, began beating her husband over the head with it, stopping only when one of their children begged her to. She then rushed her husband to the hospital to have his head injuries treated.

Embarrassed, perhaps, that a 5-foot-2-inch woman whacked his 6-foot-2-inch, 250-pound frame, the man never pressed charges against his wife.

Traffic Stop Challenge
June 21, 1973

On a hot summer night two young men who had spent hours drinking in a local tavern decided to race home in their cars. Inebriated, they had a twenty dollar bet going as to which one would arrive first. But while the men were speeding, one of their vehicles crossed over a curb killing a Wisconsin Rapids woman.

In response, I set up radar on that same road the following night. Early on, I locked in on a Crown Victoria traveling 75 miles per hour in a 40 mile-per-hour zone. I proceeded after the vehicle with red lights and siren activated until it pulled over onto the shoulder of the road. Since we were stopped on a narrow bridge, I had the driver get into the passenger seat of the squad car for his safety. Recognizing the man as Ron Adamek,* a local acquaintance, I asked him if he realized that he was driving 75 in the posted 40 zone. His response made me laugh.

"I know I was speeding," he said, "but it doesn't matter because I'm a really good driver."

Ron then gave me a critical stare. "You're not really going to write me a ticket?" he asked.

"You bet your ass I am," I answered.

With a scowl on his face, I could see Ron was pissed off. "I suppose that makes you a big, important man," he implied sarcastically. "C'mon, you're not really going to write me a ticket, are you?"

"Perhaps it would help you," I said, "if I wrote the citation for driving 69 miles per hour in a 35 zone which would save you money."

"Do whatever you want," he replied. "You can wipe your ass with that ticket if it makes you happy."

As I filled out the citation, I could see out the corner of my eye that Ron was looking me up and down, visually scrutinizing my sheriff's attire. "You think you're tough wearing that badge on your chest and carrying that gun on your side, don't you?" he asked. "I'll bet you're not so tough when you're off duty."

"You don't want to know," I replied.

Apathetically, Ron stared out the window. "See this badge right here?" I said pointing to it on my chest. "This is the only thing keeping me from kicking the absolute shit out of you right here, right now."

"Pfft, yeah right," he said. "Big talk from a real tough guy."

I asked Ron where he hung out so I could show him that I didn't fear him without my badge and gun, and that I wasn't simply hiding behind the law.

"What? You wanna fight me?" he asked in a cocky tone. "You don't have the balls."

He informed me that he would be at John and Elaine's Bar in Plover on Saturday night. Never one to walk away from a fight I agreed to meet him there.

I was off duty on Saturday and had just seeded a lawn for a residence south of Plover for some extra money. As I returned to town with my tools, I suddenly remembered that I had a date with a smart-mouthed wiseguy at a local watering hole. Pulling into the bar's parking lot, I immediately recognized Ron's car. Covered in dirt from the day's work I walked into the bar and spotted my target sitting on a barstool talking to his wife. I grabbed the back of the man's black leather jacket and pulled him off the stool. When his ass hit the ground, he jumped up with a shocked look on his face. I then seized a fistful of his shirt, threw him out the side door, and into the parking lot, pinning him against a pickup truck. Ron's face was as white as a ghost. He never thought I would show up. "Okay, here's your chance, tough guy," I told him, "start swinging." Not wanting any part of a fight, the man backed off. Suddenly, Ron's wife ran out of the bar, jumped on my back, and wrapped her arms around my neck trying to keep me from beating up her husband. I explained to the woman what had transpired earlier in the week and this was her spouse's challenge, not mine. "So get off my back!"

Ron was noticeably embarrassed since there were many people in the bar that he knew. After he apologized for giving me a hard time, I let him go. Walking back to my car, the bar patrons gave me a round of applause for standing up to the man who was widely known in the area for being a jerk.

From that day forward, Ron Adamek conveyed an unspoken respect with a smile and a nod of the head whenever he would see me around town.

An Alternate Use for Kotex

July 7, 1973

Portage County deputies were responsible for patrolling 810 square miles of largely rural geography. So we made certain to carry any equipment we might need in the trunks of our squad cars; everything from extrication equipment and additional flashlights to throw rings in case of a drowning. We also carried cases of Kotex panty liners because they made perfect bandages in instances of excessive bleeding.

Take, for example, a one-car accident that occurred while I worked traffic control at the Golden Sands Speedway about nine miles west of Plover near

Wisconsin Rapids. The night was uneventful until the stock car races ended. I directed most of the exiting traffic onto Highway 54 and then headed east to return home. While driving I spotted what appeared to be a plume of smoke ahead of me. As I got a little closer it turned out to be a cloud of dust, which drew my attention to a huge oak tree about 200 feet from the road. Wrapped around the tree was a red Mustang containing two twenty-something men. Considering the severity of the accident, I couldn't believe the men were still alive.

Heading east on Highway 54 the Mustang had been passing other vehicles at a high rate of speed. Witnesses to the accident estimated that the car was traveling at more than 100 miles per hour when it lost control, traveled through a ditch, and struck the oak tree head on. The windshield shattered back into the car causing a piece of broken glass to scalp the driver. The man's skull flesh was cut in the form of a flap that was still attached to the back of his head. So I tossed the flap into place and then applied Kotex panty liners as a bandage after wrapping the man's skull with gauze.

The passenger's-side door of the Mustang had to be forced open with a percussive response tool. The passenger, John McCodlo, was seated facing forward. His right leg, driven back under the front seat, had been twisted around the frame of the seat track. The leg had several compound fractures where the bone was broken and driven through the flesh. Deputy Art Lepak and I had to remove the seat anchors to free the man's leg. I then pulled the leg straight and applied an inflatable splint normally used on heart attack victims to force the blood in the legs toward the heart. The splint was full length with a zipper on one side and inflatable by blowing into an air valve to apply pressure. As the splint inflated, the painful screams from the victim changed to sighs of relief.

After Art and I cleared the scene and the two men were transported to Saint Michael's, I headed to the hospital myself to gather information for the officer's report. The emergency room doctor asked me who set the leg and inflated the splint. "I did," I replied thinking there was a problem. He said that the bone was stabilized so perfectly that he was able to pin it into place with no problem. Since I am nobody's doctor, it was a relief to hear. I was concerned that I might have done some harm at the scene by severing arteries or damaging nerves. Returning to the office, I submitted my incident report and retired for the evening.

Three months later while working the jail, there was a knock on the dispatch center door. Standing in the doorway on crutches was John McCodlo. I let him in and offered him a chair. John said he wanted to see me personally and thank me for saving his leg and possibly his life. We sat and talked for hours while I ran the dispatch center.

With all the difficulties that an officer encounters, gratitude such as this makes it all worthwhile.

Strange Place to Take a Nap
August 18, 1973

I met Johnny Simpson* on a muggy Saturday afternoon after receiving a call from a woman in Junction City who said there was a "strange dude" sleeping on her front lawn. Deputy Pete Thrun and I pulled up to her residence to witness a young man wearing a leather jacket lying on the ground with a rat-tail comb sticking out of his back pocket. With his Harley-Davidson motorcycle lying on its side by the curb, Johnny appeared inebriated. I asked him how much alcohol he had to drink. "Quite a bit," he replied.

"You'll have to come with us," I told him.

"You ain't man enough to take me!" he yelled.

I told Pete to open the back door of my squad car. When we lifted Johnny up on his feet, he pulled out his rat-tail comb and tried to stab me with it. Grabbing his wrist, I got a few scratches from the comb, but I was able to slap my handcuffs on him. Pete locked up his squad car and rode back to the station with me sitting in the front passenger seat. Johnny, seated right behind him in the back seat, was busy cussing up a storm. "Settle down back there," I ordered.

"Where are you taking me?" Johnny asked.

"To jail," I replied.

"The hell you are," he said as he started kicking the backs of our seats.

Johnny began to make short grunting noises as if he was trying to clear his throat. Sporting a roguish grin, he coughed up a ball of phlegm and held it on his tongue. I watched him in the rear view mirror as he pointed his mouth in my direction.

"Johnny, if you blow that slug at me it'll be the last thing you do," I told him.

Pthu! Johnny spit the phlegm onto the back of my head. Keeping my left hand on the steering wheel, I turned around and smacked him across the face with the back of my right hand. His eyes were as big as golf balls as he watched my hand approach. By the time we arrived at the jail, Johnny was bleeding profusely from his nose and mouth. Stubbornly, he refused to walk letting his legs out from under him. With Johnny's phlegm dripping from my hair onto my neck, I grabbed the man by his leather jacket and pulled him up to a standing position. Once again, he purposefully fell to the ground. So I grabbed him around the chest and dragged him across the floor. Pete, walking ahead of me, opened the elevator door and I sat Johnny down in the corner. When the man began to slouch, I realized he was unconscious from being inadvertently squeezed a little too hard.

Johnny Simpson was booked for disorderly conduct and creating a disturbance. He couldn't be charged with operating his motorcycle under the influence since Pete and I hadn't witnessed him in the act. I released the man after he paid his fines.

Several weeks after the incident, Johnny personally apologized to me for his misbehavior and we became good friends.

Emergency Surgery
September 23, 1973

On this mild, early autumn day, the sheriff's department received a call regarding a farm machinery accident. On arrival, I was shocked to find a man tangled in the power take-off of a tractor.

A local farmer had been selling shelled corn to a regional food company. The farmer used an auger to load the corn from a storage granary into the company's truck. A take-off shaft that was turned by the tractor powered the auger. The farmer reported that one of his workers, thirty-year-old Ken Millner,* had stepped too close to the shaft causing his trousers to become tangled; in the process, wrapping his leg around the shaft all the way up to the thigh. Ken was turned over multiple times, flipping through the air as his body bounced on the ground with each revolution. The farmer heard his worker's screams and rushed to shut off the tractor engine, but by that time, the man's leg was completely wound on the shaft.

Without delay, I called a surgeon and a nurse to the scene. After injecting sedatives to reduce Ken's pain the doctor proceeded to cut away the flesh one chunk at a time. He laid the pieces of flesh on surgical sheets in the hope of trying to salvage the leg and rebuild it later. A blanket was positioned so Ken couldn't see the surgical procedure. The man, conscious but nervous, began to chain smoke cigarettes until the surgery was complete. He was then loaded in a waiting ambulance and rushed to Saint Michael's where reconstruction of the leg was attempted.

The procedure failed and the man lost his leg, but he lived to tell about the horrific ordeal—one of the most gruesome I had ever seen.

Suicidal Tendencies
October 7, 1973

On a dark, overcast Sunday morning Deputy Vince Wanta and I responded to a call in Junction City in which a woman claimed that her husband, Arek,* had committed suicide.

According to the wife, Arek had been suffering mental problems for many years. She had gone to church early that morning leaving her husband alone in the house. When she returned he was hanging from a noose in the garage. Sure enough, when we reported to the property we found a man suspended from a rope in a dusty, crowded corner. Next to the body, we noticed a piece of lumber braced up against the wall as though it was used as a stepping device.

Vince reached up to turn Arek's body so it would face us. When he did, a cat jumped on his shoulder causing him nearly to have a heart attack. The married couple's pet had been sitting inconspicuously on a wooden rafter licking blood from the dead man's face.

Arek had attempted suicide three times. The first attempt was by way of carbon monoxide poisoning but his car ran out of gas before the deed could be accomplished. He then retrieved a .410 shotgun from a cabinet inside his house and walked back to the garage. He put the weapon under his chin and pulled the trigger blowing off the entire right side of his face. The bullet had shattered the man's jaw and his right eyeball was missing from its socket. Yet he was still alive. Blood and flesh could be seen dripping from the rafters in the garage above where Arek was standing. Apparently, the man touched his face as he stumbled around the garage. He placed his hands on his car for support and left a number of bloody palm prints on the vehicle.

Undeterred, he then went to the corner of the garage, threw a rope over a rafter, and braced a 2 x 4 against the wall. He tied the rope around his neck, walked up the piece of lumber, and then stepped off, successfully killing himself.

Consensual Sex or Forcible Rape?

October 20, 1973

A young woman walked into the emergency room at Saint Michael's claiming to have been raped during a fraternity party at the University of Wisconsin-Stevens Point. She said that after consuming a few drinks she was beginning to feel drunk. That's when a man at the party allegedly took her into a bedroom and sexually assaulted her. Adamant about the attack, the woman said she could identify her assailant.

During questioning of other female students who attended the party it was learned that the sexual contact between the man and the woman was consensual. Two girls in attendance said the accuser "had an eye for the guy" the entire evening and had informed him that she couldn't wait to go to bed with him. When the man was questioned, he said that the encounter started with a simple hug and a kiss until the girl grabbed his genitals and pulled him into the bedroom. She then stripped off all of her clothes and crawled into bed.

Upon further investigation, it was learned that once the woman sobered up after the party she became embarrassed by what had transpired. So she decided to falsely accuse the man of forcible rape rather than face ridicule from her peers.

The male student was cleared, but he could have gone to prison if witnesses had not come forward.

He Who Laughs Last...

November 11, 1973

While patrolling east of Polonia I was dispatched to an auto accident with injuries about a half mile away. Rounding Highway 66 at the Polonia curve doing 90 miles per hour, a deer suddenly leaped out at my squad car. It struck the windshield before sliding across the roof taking out the beacons and siren. The animal's hooves also smashed both of my headlights. Despite the banged up car I was still able to make it to the accident scene.

Two men and a woman that suffered injuries were transported to Saint Michael's, and in twenty minutes, the scene was cleared. Arriving moments earlier, Sergeant Bob Check approached me and said, "Hey 'Crash,' you can ride with me since your squad car is totaled." Not only was the vehicle in bad shape it had also overheated. Though I was hardly responsible for the condition of the squad car, it was still an embarrassing situation. So I got into Bob's car and rode without saying a word.

The dispatcher then called the sergeant to advise him of an accident with injuries located north of Stevens Point. Speeding through town to get there, a caution light came on as we traveled on Division Street just prior to passing the fire department. The driver of the car in front of us abruptly braked when he saw the caution light. Sergeant Check braked as well, but not fast enough, slamming the car from behind. "So tell me, Bob—who has the last laugh?" I asked sardonically.

Later that year, when the Portage County Sheriff's Department held its annual Christmas party, Sergeant Check mockingly received a plaque for helping control the deer population in the county since he had hit about seven of the animals during the year—more than anyone else on the force.

The following summer Sergeant Check was driving his personal car to a mandatory pistol shoot at the county range. Simultaneously, I drove to the range in my squad car to complete my qualification rounds. As I pulled through the gate at the entrance, I came upon a deep pothole of water and slowed down briefly to decide on which side I should drive. Suddenly, I felt a jolt from behind. I got out of the car and approached the driver that struck my vehicle. Sure enough, it was Sergeant Check. "What the hell did you stop for?" he asked. The infuriated look on his reddened face told me he was none too pleased.

After we shot our rounds, I went to the dispatch center at the county jail to check on any new activities. As I stepped off the elevator, I saw the sergeant on the phone speaking to his insurance agent. "Hello, Jim? It's me, Bob."

I laughed so hard I nearly wet my pants.

Slippery When Wet, Pt. 2

November 27, 1973

Working patrol on a cold, damp night, I was dispatched to a two-vehicle accident on U.S. Highway 10 near Amherst. Snowing for about an hour before I got the call, the roads in the area had become wet and treacherous. I arrived at the scene to find a Peterbilt tractor-trailer loaded with potatoes pulled off to the shoulder of the road. The truck's driver, Ben Golomski, a 6-foot-3, 230-pound man in his mid-sixties, was crying like a baby pointing to the Chevy Impala he had struck. He knew its driver had been seriously injured.

I approached the damaged vehicle to find forty-year-old Brad Bolodak* lying face down on its hood. Checking for a pulse, I found that the man was alive. An ambulance soon arrived and he was stabilized on a body board for transport to Saint Michael's.

Now came the investigation to determine what happened.

Ben said he was traveling east on Highway 10 down the long gradual decline when he saw headlights approaching a half-mile away in the westbound lane. The Impala's left turn signal came on at the entrance to the Tomorrow River Supper Club in Amherst. The truck driver began to brake gently when he noticed the signal. Suddenly, Brad changed his mind and returned to his own lane causing Ben to lock the Peterbilt's brakes. With its high clearance, the tractor-trailer passed over the Impala ripping off its hood and roof. Considering the damage to the vehicle, it was hard to believe that Brad was still alive.

I finished the investigation at the scene and had a towing service remove the car. I then headed to the hospital to speak with the medical staff as to the condition of the driver. Dr. Clarence "Mike" Klasinski, one of the best orthopedic surgeons in America, told me that the man's legs were so badly mangled he had the hospital maintenance man build two wooden troughs to hold them together until he could make a decision as to what to do surgically. The man was lying on his back attached to a breathing machine. His feet were pointing down even though the rest of his body was face up.

The many surgeries performed by Dr. Klasinski to save his legs failed but the man lived.

"Do You Know Who I Am?"

September 8, 1974

Early in 1960, Andy Griffith stepped out of his police car in an episode of *The Danny Thomas Show* (known as *Make Room for Daddy* during its first three seasons) to hand a speeding ticket to Thomas's character, a nightclub entertainer named Danny Williams.

"Kindly take a look at my name," Williams said as he handed Griffith his license. "You'll discover that I'm somebody."

"I knew that the minute I laid eyes on you," Griffith said as he looked over the license. "Yes sir, I've never seen a car yet that wasn't being driven by *somebody.*"

As the scene progressed, Griffith continued to put Williams in his place to make sure he knew who was in charge.

To that point, I've always believed that the public should respect law enforcement. But such respect had to be earned not demanded.

For instance, a car crash took place on Highway 10 in Amherst that cost a fifty-four-year-old woman her life. A thirty-three-year-old man traveling at about 80 miles per hour in a posted 55 zone collided head on with the woman's vehicle killing her instantly. So the following day around mid-afternoon, I set up radar near the accident location. Within thirty minutes, a black Cadillac sped through at 80 miles per hour. I wasted no time in stopping the car.

"I pulled you over because you were going 80 in a 55 zone," I said to the driver, a mid-fifties-looking man.

"Isn't this a 65 zone?" he asked.

"No it's a 55 zone," I replied. "And regardless, you'd still be speeding."

The man looked at me as if I was the dumbest person on earth. "Do you know who I am?" he asked arrogantly.

I told him that I did since his name was on his driver's license.

Decked out in an impeccable suit and tie, the man, who happened to be the president of a local bank, proceeded to lecture me about bothering him when murderers were walking the streets. It appeared that I was unworthy of his presence.

"A bank president doesn't carry any more weight than a mill worker," I stated.

"You should be proud of yourself," he said as I wrote out his ticket. "I hope this fills your monthly quota."

"My quota was filled yesterday," I countered with a smile. "This ticket I'm writing for the hell of it!"

The banker held the ticket in both hands as though he was going to tear it up and throw it back at me. "I wouldn't do that if I were you," I said, "unless you want to face additional charges for littering and disorderly conduct."

Thinking wisely, he crumpled the ticket and threw it onto his passenger seat. With a pout on his face, he drove away.

(For the record, the Portage County Sheriff's Department never imposed ticket quotas on its law enforcement officers.)

Girl Gone Wild

September 21, 1974

"My daughter has gone off the deep end again," said the father who called the sheriff's department. When Deputy Pete Thrun and I reported to the man's residence just north of Stevens Point, he stated that his twenty-five-year-old daughter Anna,* who had been institutionalized at a mental facility just one year before, was on a rampage. She was breaking dishes, kicking holes in the walls, and repeatedly screaming, "They're coming to get me!"

Try as we may, Pete and I couldn't convince Anna to calm down. So we decided she was a candidate for an emergency mental commitment—not to mention a straitjacket. A tremendously strong woman, it took all the muscle Pete and I could muster just to get handcuffs on her. After nearly ten minutes, we were able to strap her into the back seat of the squad car. We were then on our way to the Norwood Health Center in Marshfield, a forty-five mile drive.

During the transport, Anna began to growl like an angry dog. Looking in the rearview mirror, I could see that the woman had locked her teeth together and was staring intently at Pete. She asked the deputy if he wanted to have sex with her to which he simply shook his head "no" in response. Anna then calmed and began to talk to us. She claimed that her father had sexually abused her since she was a young girl. She also said he had abused her two older sisters. When we arrived at Norwood, I conveyed to one of the doctors what Anna had told us during the transport. After speaking with the woman and performing a physical examination, the doctor believed she was lying.

Anna's claims of sexual abuse were eventually turned over to investigators who found they were without merit. Consequently, the woman remained at the mental health facility.

Racial Incident on the Campus of UWSP

October 10, 1974

In the late 1960s and early 1970s, racial tensions continued to run high in populated urban areas of the Midwest such as Milwaukee and Chicago. Although not as newsworthy, such tensions also existed in more rural areas.

During this time, the University of Wisconsin—Stevens Point had a number of minority students who were accepted into the community no differently from the white students.

However, there was a situation where local auto mechanic Hubert Kozlow* had joined a friend of his for a beer at one of the bars on the school's campus. While taking his first sip of brew, he got into a heated argument with Michael Stewart,* a black student who happened to be at the bar with a white girl. After words were exchanged, including some racial slurs, Hubert and his friend decided to leave. As they walked toward the door, Michael followed the auto mechanic close behind. Sensing the man's presence, Hubert turned around and the two began arguing again. As they did, Michael punched the mechanic in his chest causing him to fall to his knees. The man then bolted through the door and headed toward his dormitory. Hubert suddenly realized that the pain he felt wasn't the result of a punch but from a stab wound. A pocketknife with a three-inch blade had penetrated his chest and pierced a lung, missing his heart by less than an inch. Bleeding profusely, his friend helped him into his car and rushed him to Saint Michael's about three blocks away. The doctors that tended to Hubert said he was lucky the incident took place so close to the hospital and that his friend wasted no time in getting him there, otherwise, he would have bled to death. After emergency surgery and a week of recovery, the auto mechanic survived his life-threatening wound.

Since neither Hubert nor and his friend could positively identify the assailant no charges were filed.

Murder or Suicide?

November 14, 1974

Twenty-two-year-old Plover resident Andrew Gordon* parked his car on a short, dead-end service road just off County Highway DB stretching out a quarter mile into the Portage County countryside. The young man then attached a vacuum cleaner hose to the tail pipe of the vehicle, ran it through the rear driver's-side window, and stuffed rags around it to keep the carbon monoxide inside. In a matter of minutes, he was dead.

Andrew's mother was adamant that her son was dealing drugs and that his death wasn't suicide, but murder at the hands of drug dealers or their accomplices. Many Portage County residents considered the man suspicious, a loner who typically avoided social interaction. But he didn't have a criminal record.

There was no indication of any struggle or forceful means of keeping Andrew in the car. He was sitting behind the wheel with his head hanging back on the seat, his body covered with dark blue and red blotches from the coagulation of blood mixed with carbon monoxide.

Despite his mother's assertions, it appeared that Andrew's death was a suicide. After dusting the car for prints, I found none except for the young man's. There was no sign of a scuffle and there were no bruises on the man's body.

6
POLICE CHIEF
STORIES

To insure the adoration of a theorem
for any length of time, faith is not enough,
a police force is needed as well.

—Albert Camus

Building a Police Department
from Scratch

In early May 1975, the Village of Plover announced the creation of its own police department. Since my family lived in Plover, my wife and I decided that I should apply for the position of police chief. Going into the interview, I was nervous as hell. My competition, which included assistant chiefs of police and police captains from other local departments in central and eastern Wisconsin, had me sweating under the collar. But on May 16, after a lengthy and grueling process, the village selected me as its first chief of police.

The Plover Police Department was built from the ground up. From the day I was hired I had no police officers or occupational guidelines. I didn't even have an office. The board of directors assisted me in purchasing and equipping a squad car, designing a uniform, creating an insignia, establishing ordinances, purchasing side arms, and, yes, finding an office from which to work. My office would be equipped with military surplus furniture, rusty metal desks and file drawers, and old dilapidated chairs. Soon enough, I posted office hours as to my public availability as well as my schedule for street patrol.

In spring 1976, I hired the first Plover police officer, Roger Zebro, to assist me with patrol duties. Within three years, the Plover police force grew to four full-time officers.

"Buford"

July 12, 1975

Returning home at 2 A.M. from an exhausting shift, I went straight to bed for some much needed rest. In the midst of some serious REM sleep, a telephone ring awakened me at 3:30 A.M. The caller, a female speaking in a shaken voice, said there was a large group of inebriated townsfolk in a local restaurant after closing time and they had started a fight with some of the remaining patrons. I pulled on a pair of old, beat up Levis, hopped in my squad car, and rushed to the scene, which, thankfully, was only a few miles away.

Walking through the front door, I was shocked at the condition of the restaurant. Broken chairs, tables, and ketchup bottles covered the floor. As punches flew, there were many bloody faces. I was able to restrain six of the twelve brawlers and place them under arrest before Deputy Ray Potocki arrived from the sheriff's department to assist. The scene took more than an hour to clear. By the time I returned to the office, I was covered with blood, cuts, and bruises.

A few days later, a group of villagers visited my office and presented me with a nightstick they had created by turning a maple block on a lathe and then staining it in an antique finish. Placing the stick in my hand, they proclaimed me "Buford" in honor of the movie *Walking Tall* featuring Buford Pusser, a small-town sheriff in Tennessee. Pusser was always outnumbered, outgunned, and undermanned but he never gave in or gave up, gaining the respect of the local populace.

It's Just a Game of Pool

July 19, 1975

Chances are you've heard the old maxim, "The best way to win a fight is to avoid a fight." Although I don't condone fights, sometimes they can't be avoided. After all, there is a philistine side to all humans, and on occasion, it rears its ugly head. It growls, behaves recklessly, shatters inanimate objects, and gives or receives a few broken bones.

While patrolling in Plover on a hot sunny afternoon, I was dispatched to a fight at a local watering hole called Coney Island. The bar had a front door that faced the parking lot and a back door that faced the road. On this day, the back door happened to be open due to the sultry weather. As I drove by and looked inside, I saw a number of people taking swings at each other next to a billiards table. It appeared that due to an argument over a game of pool local barroom ruffian Bruce Bauman* had started a fight. Clearly inebriated, Bruce was screaming like a wild man at the other patrons. He was also holding a wooden cue stick like a baseball bat looking to hit someone.

Pulling off to the edge of the road, I exited my car and ran through the back door just in time to witness Bruce swing his cue stick at the face of a ter-rified patron. With my right hand, I reached out and caught the stick in mid-air. I then grabbed the goon by the back of the neck and spun him around facing away from me. At 240 pounds of solid muscle, Bruce was quite a bruiser. But I was able to pull his left arm behind his back and run him face first into an adjacent wall—unaware there was a payphone hanging there. All but knocked out, the man slid slowly to the floor leaving behind a long streak of blood on the phone and the old, shabby paneling that covered the wall.

Had Bruce made contact with the cue stick the patron could have been ser-iously injured, even killed. So I hardly felt sorry for him kissing the payphone. Neither did the two dozen or so patrons in the bar who offered me a standing ovation for my actions pleased to see the feared man get what he deserved. Bruce was notorious for being a badass who struck fear into the local popu-lace, particularly at bars where the patrons just wanted to hang out and shoot pool with friends.

All Lawbreakers
Should Be This Respectful
July 27, 1975

Patrolling Highway 54, I met a car headed west accelerating at a fast rate of speed. I turned around, activated my lights, and gave pursuit. I finally caught up to the car, an orange 1970 Plymouth Road Runner, near the Plover vil-lage limits.

The driver handed me his license and immediately apologized for having exceeded the 45 miles per hour speed limit. According to protocol, I had him step out of the car to determine his stability.

"Do you realize how fast you were going?" I asked.

"My car doesn't run well at low speeds, sir," the man replied. "It's kinda sluggish. So when I reach about forty miles an hour or so I have a habit of gunning it a little."

I pointed to a deer-crossing sign a few yards away and told him that many people have been injured, even killed, after hitting the animals, particularly at high speeds.

"I assure you, sir, that it won't happen again," he said, "if you'll just give me a break this time."

"Do you know a speeding ticket on the driving record of an eighteen-year-old man would result in points on his license and increased insurance rates?"

"Yes sir, I do," he responded. "That's why I'm asking for forgiveness."

I told the man that I knew his father and he would not be happy to learn that his son doesn't respect traffic laws. Nonetheless, I decided to forego a citation in favor of a written warning since I felt the young man had learned his lesson.

A few days later, the same man, Sidney Rzentkowski, visited me in my Plover office to thank me for the written warning I had given him. He then asked if he could take a picture of me standing next to my squad car. Two weeks later he came back to the office and handed me a pencil sketch of the picture he had taken—an impressive piece of artwork.

A respectable young man, Sidney and I became good friends and remain so today. Sometimes a stern discussion can be more effective than writing a citation for every violation that an officer encounters.

Maybe Pizza Isn't
the Healthiest Meal

August 3, 1975

Patrolling Plover on Porter Road near U.S. Highway 51 I observed a man and a woman, perhaps in their mid-fifties, straddling their bicycles at the fence along the highway. They were eating a pizza while watching the traffic go by, enjoying a beautiful summer Sunday afternoon.

Suddenly, I saw the man's body start to jerk up and down. A few seconds later, he fell to the ground and the woman he was with began to scream. I jumped out of the squad car and ran to assist them. Thinking that the man was choking on his pizza, I applied the Heimlich maneuver but to no avail. I checked his vitals while he lay motionless but found none. Turned out the man was having a heart attack. I cleared his mouth and airway, rolled him onto his back, and began mouth-to-mouth resuscitation and heart compression simultaneously, trying my best to induce purposeful movements. Meanwhile, the woman ran to a nearby house where she called for an ambulance. With the palms of my hands I pressed into the man's sternum with the entire weight of my 248-pound body; three compressions to one breath of air, being as careful as I could not to snap off the xiphoid process right into his heart. The last thing I wanted to do was accidentally kill a man whose life I was trying save. The temperature that day, a sizzling ninety-three degrees, had me sweating bullets making my efforts to save the man that much tougher.

When the ambulance arrived about ten minutes later, I hopped inside and provided uninterrupted resuscitation to the man in transport to Saint Michael's. A doctor ran into the emergency room and told me to continue with the same rhythm while he prepared the shocking equipment. I then took a step back as he applied cardiac paddles.

My attempt to save the man lasted more than thirty minutes. Physically, I was exhausted. My entire uniform was soaked with sweat and I had difficulty catching my breath. The bodily exertion was unbearable considering how much pressure had to be applied to the man's sternum just to get it close to his heart.

Unfortunately, the man didn't survive. But in appreciation of my efforts his female companion threw her arms around me extending thanks for how hard I tried to save his life.

Tragedy in the Courtroom

August 20, 1975

One of my obligations as Plover police chief was to appear in court at 10 A.M. every Monday to present ordinance and traffic violations. With some of my Plover officers and those from the Stevens Point Police Department, I stood on the second floor courtroom located on Strongs Avenue in downtown Stevens Point listening to Judge Fred Fleischauer impose fines and punishments

On this morning, the judge read a citation from a Stevens Point police officer against seventy-five-year-old Barney Foreman* who ran a red light. Barney wanted to plead "no contest" but not before telling the judge his version of what happened. Surprisingly, the man's story was compelling enough to sway the court's opinion. "After considering the circumstances," the judge said, "it appears you took every precaution you could. I hereby find you not guilty."

Just as Judge Fleischauer prepared to bring down the gavel and dismiss the case, Barney began to sway from side to side. He then forcefully vomited and his head dropped to the table in front of him. His face turned blue and he fell off his chair and onto the floor. The man was in the throes of a massive heart attack.

Stevens Point Police Officer Jim Rogers knelt at Barney's side and felt for a pulse. Feeling none, he turned to me and asked, "Can you perform CPR?" Rogers was known in the department not only for being apprehensive about blood but for having a weak stomach in general. So I knelt down next to the civilian as he regurgitated his breakfast. Reaching for my handkerchief, I wiped the vomit from his mouth and started mouth-to-mouth resuscitation. In a matter of seconds, a normal color returned to his face and he regained a pulse.

Minutes later, an ambulance arrived and Barney was loaded onto a stretcher and rolled into a nearby elevator. However, he began to experience another heart attack. Again, I performed CPR on the man. "He has a pulse!" the ambulance attendant yelled. The man gasped and began to breathe during transport to the hospital.

Before returning to the courtroom to present citations to Judge Fleischauer, I made a beeline for the men's room to gargle Barney's vomit from my mouth and wash off the streaks of excess debris that had dribbled down my chin onto my shirt. Out of respect, I reported to the courtroom as quickly as I could.

The judge thanked me for my efforts in tending to Barney, and I began presenting my traffic citations. Moments later, the court bailiff handed a note to the judge that said the civilian was alive and in stable condition. But shortly after, he suffered another heart attack. The bailiff then approached the judge and whispered in his ear that Barney had not survived the third attack. The judge ordered the people in the courtroom to bow their heads in a moment of silence to honor the man's memory.

After hearing that Barney died, Judge Fleischauer shook his head. With a look of regret he said, "You know Dan, I think we should have kept that man right here," inferring, somewhat tongue in cheek, that he might have lived if he had remained in the courtroom as opposed to going to the hospital.

Rogue ROTC Colonel
December 10, 1975

On a frigid late afternoon, I heard a call for assistance in the Village of Park Ridge, a suburb of Stevens Point. The dispatcher reported that a man with a shotgun had fired a few bullets in the direction of his son inside his home. Immediately, two deputies responded to the scene. After stepping out of their squad car, they were promptly met by gunfire. One of the shots struck the right side of the vehicle, causing the deputies to dive for cover behind a hedge-row.

Patrolling Plover only a short distance from the area, I responded to the call for assistance. Arriving at the scene, I saw the squad car abandoned in the middle of the street with both doors open and its engine running. I parked on the shoulder about 200 feet from the residence and took out my 12-gauge semi-automatic shotgun. The weapon had a flashlight molded on top serving as an illuminated sight. Walking toward the idled squad car, I ordered the man to exit his house unarmed. He answered me through a front window with a 12-gauge slug that blew out the spotlight of my parked squad car.

Then all went silent.

About a minute later, the garage door opened. Against a bracing wind, a tall, powerful-looking man began walking in my direction holding a shotgun at port arms. He hurled obscenities at me when I yelled for him to drop his weapon. When he approached the driver's-side door of the idled squad car, he promptly turned his back to me. "You've never seen combat like I have, you bastard!" he shouted over his shoulder. "I've killed men in Vietnam! You can't shoot me, *you've* never killed anyone! Besides, you don't have the guts to shoot a man in the back, you motherfucker!" The man then jumped into the squad car and slammed the door shut. Rolling down the driver's-side window, he thrust out the barrel of his shotgun. He then shifted the car into reverse and gunned the engine. About thirty feet from him, I sought safety behind a pine tree with my weapon at the ready. I didn't want to shoot the man at that range because I knew what a 12-gauge shotgun loaded with 00 buck-shot would do to him. Suddenly, I heard Sheriff Nick Check's voice on my radio. "Whatever you do Dan," he said, "don't let him leave with that squad car!"

"Not to worry, Sheriff," I replied. "This guy isn't going anywhere."

I pleaded with the man to step out of the squad car and drop the gun. Instead, he attempted to use the car to flee. I had to stop the man, but I didn't have the heart to kill him. So I leveled my weapon on the rear tire and fired, shredding it to pieces. I then fired at the cap of the gas tank causing fuel to spill out of the back of the car. I expected the vehicle to explode, but thankfully, it didn't. The next shot I fired was near the man's head through the rear passenger's-side window thinking the resulting vibration would shock him into submission. But all it did was shatter the windows of the squad car. Again, the man pushed the shotgun barrel out of the driver's-side window in my direction. I knew the last target was the left side of his head. Under my icy breath, I asked God to forgive me as I drew a bead on him. But the man noticed the light in his face and lunged for the passenger's seat just as I squeezed the trigger. A few seconds later, faint moans emanated from the car. Walking out from behind the pine tree, I saw the man lying on the passenger's seat on his right side. I yelled for him to push his shotgun out the window and step out of the car. He gradually propped himself up and carefully pushed the weapon through the window until it fell to the ground. He then opened the door and walked to the front of the squad car with his hands raised. Just then, Wisconsin State Trooper Wayne Miesner arrived to assist. During the course of the incident, I was in communication with Wayne on my portable radio keeping him well informed of what was happening. Together we tackled the man to the ground dislocating his elbow. He was then transported to Saint Michael's in handcuffs where he was treated for his injury.

The man was arraigned in circuit court on the following Monday. While the judge read the charges to him, an Army general accompanied by two military police officers marched into the courtroom. They approached the judge with an order to take the man into custody to be tried in a military tribunal. As it turned out, he was a Reserve Officer Training Corps colonel with a drinking problem. The judge read the order and released the man to the military police who led him away in chains.

Later that evening I apologized to Nick Check for having destroyed the squad car. The vehicle was one of two belonging to the force that had been painted with a gaudy design for the upcoming American Bicentennial celebration in July 1976. The cars, though mostly white, had blue roofs and red doors that prompted plenty of stares from bystanders whenever they passed through town.

"Don't worry about it," Nick said with a laugh. "I hated that freakin' car anyway!"

Officer Down

December 20, 1975

While patrolling Plover on a cold, moonless night, I received a call from the Sheriff's dispatcher around 11:30 P.M. that Roger Wrycza had been shot. Wrycza, the police chief of Almond-Pine Grove, a small rural town at the south end of Portage County, had apparently taken a bullet after pulling over an erratic driver in a yellow pickup truck. I responded to the call after getting a full description of the vehicle, which, after leaving the scene, was headed in my direction. Angry that a fellow law enforcement officer was shot, I rolled down the passenger's-side window of my squad car ready to shoot the gutless bastard with the automatic shotgun lying next to me on the seat. As it turned out, I never met the vehicle head on.

Approaching Almond-Pine Grove, I could see a squad car on the side of the road with its beacons flashing. The car belonged to a police officer from Plainfield, a small village just across the border in Waushara County. The officer had heard the dispatcher's call and reported to the scene. I also noticed Roger's squad car with its beacons shot out. Positioned between the two squad cars was the yellow pickup truck. Not knowing what to expect I grabbed my shotgun with its mounted light and prepared for a shootout.

I pulled over to the shoulder and stepped out of my squad car. With shotgun in hand, I witnessed the Plainfield officer squatting in front of his car—a good thing, since if he had been standing I might have shot him in haste. Sitting on the ground next to him was the driver of the pickup truck. Wearing handcuffs and held at gunpoint by the officer, he was leaning back against the right front wheel of Roger's squad car with a bullet wound to his knee. I asked the officer where Chief Wrycza was. Pointing to a trail of blood, he said he ran across a roadside ditch and into a pine plantation through two feet of snow. I couldn't help but have visions of the man lying in the woods bleeding to death.

It was now midnight. With my flashlight, I followed a long trail of blood that started narrow but grew wider with every few yards. Eventually, the trail led to a farmhouse. After knocking on the door, a stone-faced middle-aged woman greeted me holding three clean white towels in her right hand and a blood-soaked towel in her left hand. "He's in the bedroom down the hallway," she said. As I approached the room, I saw that the door was closed. "Roger, it's Dan," I called out. "I'm coming in." I opened the door and stepped slowly into the unlit room. Not wanting to startle the man, I shined a small flashlight in my face so he could see who was approaching. Sitting on a bed in the corner against the wall was the Almond-Pine Grove police chief. Wide-eyed and frightened, he held his revolver with the hammer back in his shaking hands pointing it right at my head. "That son of a bitch shot me," he said quietly. "We apprehended the suspect," I countered. "And there's an ambulance on the way. Everything's going to be okay." I told him to put his weapon down and take a deep breath. It took a few moments, but he placed the gun on the bed and then lowered his head in obvious pain. After taking off Roger's gun belt, I witnessed his gunshot wound. The bullet had entered his stomach and exited through his back. Had the shot been centered a little more the police chief would have been paralyzed. The ambulance arrived moments later and medics placed my friend on a stretcher, loading him inside. I jumped in to join them and we were off to Saint Michael's.

Since Roger remained conscious during the twenty-minute ride to Stevens Point, I was able to question him about the incident. He told me that while patrolling Highway 51 he spotted a yellow pickup truck coming at him in the other lane swerving from side to side so badly it nearly hit his squad car head on. He quickly turned his car around and began pursuit, and in a few seconds, the truck pulled over. Roger approached the driver's side window and asked the young man inside for his license. After fumbling through his wallet, he handed it over. The police chief realized that the driver was under the influence of alcohol, drugs, or both. He also witnessed what appeared to be a .38 Special lying on the passenger's-side floor. He told the man to remain seated as he returned to the squad car to call in his license and request backup. Just then, Roger looked up and saw the man walking toward his car with gun in hand. The chief opened the door and stepped outside ordering the man to stop and drop the weapon. In response, the man shot Roger in the stomach and kept walking toward him. The chief shot back with his own .38 caliber revolver, grazing the man's left knee, and then ran to the rear of the squad car for protection. The suspect then opened the door of the vehicle and climbed inside compelling Roger to flee to the farmhouse.

Convicted of attempted murder the suspect was sentenced to four years in prison. But he was paroled after serving only two years.

Almond-Pine Grove Police Chief Roger Wrycza fully recovered from his wounds after several surgeries. But the experience proved traumatizing to where he was not able to return to law enforcement. Subsequently, he was elected as county clerk where he worked until he retired.

Tackle from Behind

July 10, 1976

While patrolling Plover on a muggy Saturday evening, Officer Roger Zebro witnessed a vehicle driving erratically. He proceeded to pull it over in the parking lot of a local dive called the Golden Sands Bar. Immediately, the driver, a twenty-one-year-old man, jumped out of his vehicle. Roger approached him and asked for his driver's license, but the man, who appeared to be high on drugs, refused. The officer then searched the vehicle and found a bag of marijuana. So he reached into his squad car for the radio transmitter to call for assistance with an uncontrollable suspect. Hearing the call, I immediately headed to the scene.

On arrival, I saw the young man push the door of the squad car against Roger's legs pinning them against the vehicle with such force it crushed his shins. When I jumped out of my squad car to assist, the man turned and ran from me. Chasing him through the Golden Sands parking lot and across the street the man veered to the left and ran toward a six-foot high white picket fence. Lunging at him through midair, I was able to grab the man and tackle him from behind. Simultaneously, we crashed through the fence creating a hole about four feet around. Considering we went through headfirst, it was amazing that we didn't knock ourselves out. I then handcuffed the man and led him back to the squad car.

This Isn't Vietnam

September 23, 1976

A Plover woman reported a domestic disturbance saying that her husband, a Vietnam veteran, had "completely lost it again" and was breaking dishes and furniture in their house. Roger Zebro and I took the call and we arrived at the residence minutes later. The husband, still in a rage, picked up a large lamp from his living room table and threatened to throw it at Roger. The officer pulled his nightstick from his belt ring and walked toward the man. "Oh my God, don't hit him," his wife screamed. "He has a steel plate in his head from his time in Vietnam!" She explained to us that her husband lost part of his skull due to a mortar explosion. "If he doesn't put the lamp down," Roger said as he waved his nightstick, "he's going to need a few more steel plates in his head." The man dropped the lamp and surrendered extending his hands so the officer could handcuff him. He then spent several days in the Portage County Jail.

To the best of my knowledge, there were no further incidents at the couple's residence.

Beaten Beyond Recognition

October 22, 1977

The Hazen* brothers—all nine of them—were notorious in Portage County for being badasses. Several were frequently in trouble with the law, mostly due to their penchant for bar fights.

When I reported to a shot fired in the parking lot behind the Golden Sands Bar in Plover, I happened to witness three of the Hazen brothers standing next to a pickup truck with a bullet hole in it. I also found Keith Mesick, a local man, lying in a puddle of muddy water in the middle of the lot, beaten within an inch of his life. I performed immediate first aid on the man before he was transported to Saint Michael's by ambulance.

In questioning the three Hazen brothers as to what had transpired they said that Keith threatened to shoot them due to an ongoing feud that had lingered for several months in the township of Linwood. When the brothers walked into the bar, they saw Keith sitting on a stool sipping a beer. But he quickly jumped up and ran for the back door to the parking lot. The man opened the passenger's-side door of the pickup truck, reached into the glove compartment, and pulled out a .45 caliber handgun. He then vowed to shoot the three brothers who had followed him into the parking lot. Before Keith could contemplate pulling the trigger, one of the brothers kicked the gun from his hand causing it to go off hitting the pickup truck, which happened to belong to one of other two brothers. Then all three Hazen brothers began kicking Keith, knocking him to the ground. According to several witnesses, the men used their gravel-laden boots to stomp repeatedly on his face as he lay in a puddle of beer, blood, mud, and water rendering him unconscious.

As a result, the three Hazen brothers were arrested for aggravated battery. Keith suffered several broken ribs and a broken right arm, not to mention that his head and face were barely recognizable. Shockingly, however, he was conscious. When I questioned him at the hospital the next morning, his recollection of the previous evening coincided with that of the witnesses. I asked him to sign a complaint against the Hazen brothers but he refused saying he had no interest in pressing charges, that he would handle the matter his way. I cautioned the man that he would face charges if he attempted to take justice into his own hands.

To the best of my knowledge, there was no retaliation.

It's worth noting that several years later, Keith Mesick died in a late-night motorcycle accident.

There was a sparsely marked, unlit railroad crossing off one of the side roads in Stevens Point. As Keith journeyed down the road on his bike, a train with a row of flat cars was coming though. With the nighttime darkness upon him, it was too late by the time he noticed the train. Keith locked his brakes and the motorcycle slid out from under him. The train ran over the length of the man's body slicing it perfectly in half, the impact sending his appendages flying in different directions across the Wisconsin countryside. Keith's left leg was found on the left side of the road while his head and right leg were found on the opposite side.

The following morning, I received several phone calls from people who lived in the area saying that they wanted to file charges against the Stevens Point Police Department. When I asked them why they said they had found numerous body parts strewn along the railroad tracks. They reported finding "an ear over here," and "an eyeball over there." They were angry that the police didn't do a better job of cleaning up the scene. But because the accident happened late at night at a location with virtually no lights the police couldn't do as thorough of a job cleaning the area as they would have liked. It was also possible that several squad cars might have been parked over some of the remains and the officers never noticed them.

Everybody Pulled His Weight

1978-1981

The Shantytown Bionic Polacks rope pull team was a group of men that got together to compete in a sport that was becoming popular in central Wisconsin, particularly at county fairs and weekend church picnics. The ten-man team was made up of block layers, farmers, masons, construction workers—and one chief of police. Chet and Bev's, a small tavern located in Shantytown, became our sponsor. Its owners, Chet and Bev Stanczyk, paid our entry fees and provided us with a place to work out, practice, and celebrate after victories.

Our Bionic Polacks team competed for three years and was undefeated through its second and third years of competition. Across the upper Midwest, we became the team to beat. All told, we lost only three matches.

The local rope pull association set up a regional contest inviting teams from Wisconsin, Minnesota, Iowa, and Illinois to take place at Lake Pacawa in Plover. After each division completed its pulls, Chet and Bev learned that Iowa had a super heavyweight team called the Junk Yard Dogs. The most feared team in the region, it had no competition to pull against. So the bar owners personally challenged the team, which together weighed about 3,600 pounds, to pull against our middleweight team for a prize of $500. The Junk Yard Dogs gladly accepted. "You must be out of your mind," I told Chet. "We have a great team, but the Dogs have never been beaten!"

"Perhaps," he replied, "but I watch you guys practice by pulling trucks and tractors. I know you can beat them. I have faith in you."

* * *

The match, which took place on July 4, 1978—a sweltering 95-degree day, would prove to be the most difficult in our pulling career.

When the Junk Yard Dogs arrived, we discovered they were voracious eaters who liked to eat tons of grilled chicken—nonstop, for hours. One of their team members, a burly, thirty-something man, sat down at a picnic table and consumed an entire chicken and a six-pack of beer in less than ten minutes.

On the opposite end of the rope, the Bionic Polacks weighed in at 2,250 pounds. Anchoring the team was Norbert Wierzba, the boy I hung from a tree in elementary school. At 259 pounds, Norbert, no longer a little kid, was instrumental in our team's success.

During the match two ambulances and a number of emergency medical technicians stood by to render first aid and oxygen to those that needed it. Good thing, since one of the Iowa pullers possessed so much power in his legs he splintered his lower left shin to where the bone protruded through the tongue of his high-top sneaker.

The Shantytown Bionic Polacks emerged victorious, but several pullers needed oxygen to stay conscious toward the end and a few needed transport to Saint Michael's for the treatment of minor injuries.

After defeating the Junk Yard Dogs, our team went undefeated through the regional matchups, putting an end to rope pulling competition in central Wisconsin.

Even though the Bionic Polacks were a rag tag bunch of guys sponsored by a tiny local country bar, seldom was seen a team that could beat us.

7
Becoming Sheriff

*Justice will always prevail as
far as I'm concerned.*
—Clayton Moore

Before the advent of the internet in the early 1990s, town gossip was the original social media, particularly in small communities.

Such as when a village board member came to my office after a meeting on March 10, 1978 to tell me he had been hearing rumors that I might be considering a run for the sheriff's office. "Are you looking for higher pay?" he asked. "If so, I can ask the board to approve a raise for you." I answered that I had given the position of sheriff some thought and would let him know of my decision. My wife and I had many late night conversations as to the chance I would be taking since I already had a job for life as police chief if I wanted. Plus, I wouldn't have to worry about reelection every two years. She suggested that I check with the village board as to what they were willing to pay.

In the end, the salary didn't really matter. Deep down inside the decision was already made.

Election 1978

My decision to run for sheriff of Portage County actually started in the fall of 1976. There was an election that, naturally, I didn't pay much attention to since I was busy performing my duties as Plover police chief. But the Wednesday after the sheriff's election, village clerk Mary Sommers walked into my office with some documents in her hand. "Dan, I have something interesting to show you," she said.

"What's that, Mary?" She showed me the results of the election. Although the incumbent, Nick Check, had no opposition, the citizens of Plover wrote my name on ballots 202 times.

"I would give this some serious thought if I were you," Mary said with a smile. "It seems that people appreciate the job you're doing as chief of police."

I talked to my wife about it. "I think you're ridiculous," she said. "You'd be taking a huge risk. You've just started building the police department in Plover."

"The people I've talked to said they'd be happy to share me with Portage County," I replied. "They want me to duplicate what I did in Plover."

On May 5, 1978, I walked into the county courthouse to file my candidacy. As I approached the clerk's office to fill out the requisite paperwork, I happened to bump into Sheriff Nick Check in the hallway. We proceeded to exchange pleasantries. "Hi, Dan," the sheriff said.

"Hi Nick," I responded.

"What brings you here?" he asked.

"I'm here to file for my candidacy."

"Oh, for county clerk?"

"No, I'm filing to run against *you*, Nick."

For several awkward moments, he just stood there and stared me in the face. "Against *me*, really?" he asked. "Are you kidding?"

"No, I'm not kidding," I replied, "I'm running against you for sheriff."

"Alright, then," he said with a shocked look on his face. "Let the best man win."

Soon after, I started acquiring the 500 signatures that I needed to make my candidacy official. The following week, I was humbled to turn in more than 1,500.

*　*　*

As my campaign for sheriff began, I started contacting my close friends for input. Their responses were the same: If what you accomplished in Plover could be shared with the entire county we will help you try. I knew the incumbent, Nick Check, would be tough to beat. Plus, I had a great responsibility as police chief requiring grueling hours. *When would I find the time to run a countywide election campaign?* I thought.

My first point of order was to establish a campaign committee. I put together a handful of supporters, mostly close friends, who began planning a grass roots campaign. It was exciting, yet tiring. I worked my regular schedule as police chief and then hit the campaign trail during evenings and weekends. Since my salary supported my family and paid monthly bills, I couldn't afford to take a leave of absence to campaign full time.

My team of friends and family prepared a schedule that I tried to follow as closely as possible. It began with campaigning the villages in the outlying areas of Portage County since Nick Check lived in Stevens Point—the county seat and largest municipality. The plan was to cover the rural areas first and then hit Stevens Point just before the election so hopefully Nick wouldn't see it coming. I would simply walk the villages and stop at stores and shops, introducing myself and sharing my plans for the Portage County Sheriff's Department before moving on to the next precinct.

I stood by the rule in running for any office that a sign war should not be started unless you are certain you can win. But thankfully, many people in the county were willing to display lawn signs on my behalf. A large group of supporters then went out and covered the rest of the county with signs. As the associated printing costs became too expensive we started making the signs by hand by stenciling my name on hospital bed headboards we received as a donation from a local manufacturing company. A nearby lumber business donated the stakes that held the signs. By the end of the campaign, my supporters had flooded the city of Stevens Point and all remote areas of Portage County with brochures and lawn signs.

My supporters and I spent weekends campaigning at church picnics, parades, and county fairs. Accompanied by my wife and children I walked each event as some of my best friends followed close behind wearing T-shirts with my name printed on them.

I also walked door to door across the county introducing myself and shaking hands. Since I didn't have excess money to spend, the grass roots system of campaigning was one of the best ways to meet the public. At the time, I was still working more than fifty hours per week as the Plover police chief, so the time spent ringing doorbells was limited to late afternoons and evenings covering about five square blocks at a time.

I remember some citizens asking me what I was going to do for a living after the election implying that I had no chance to beat Nick Check. I would simply take such comments with a grain of salt and move on. In particular, I remember ringing the doorbell of a mid-70s-looking couple who, after learning my name and what I was running for, looked over my shoulder to make sure I wasn't being followed. They asked why I wasn't scared that the incumbent might have me bumped off. "I fear no man," I explained. "I never back down from a fight." Without delay, they signed my nomination papers and wished me luck pointing out that many have tried unsuccessfully to beat Nick Check. I told them that I fully intended to win the election.

I had put everything on the line. I was still running the Plover police department and was well aware of the ramifications if I were to lose.

With butterflies churning in my stomach, I was unable to hold down food during the three days leading up to the election. I was lucky to get one hour of sleep on election eve. When the day finally arrived, I didn't know what to do with myself. Time virtually stood still. It seemed like the polls would never close. Then the returns started coming in. The incumbent sheriff, Nick Check, lost all thirty-nine precincts.

Surrounded by my family and closest friends, the victory celebration lasted well into the night.

After the election, I was well into the red financially. So when an offer was extended to me in Almond-Pine Grove to fill in under contract as police chief while I still temporarily ran the police department in Plover I jumped at the chance. When I finished my shift in Plover, I would park my squad car, put on my leather jacket, and jump into the Almond-Pine Grove squad car, which I kept parked in my driveway. I then headed twelve miles south.

Every morning I was on duty I would stop at Gary's Restaurant in Bancroft, an unincorporated area within the town of Almond with a population of about 300. The staff would serve me a sticky-sweet homemade cinnamon roll eight inches in diameter and covered in heavy frosting. They would put two pats of butter on it and then throw it in the microwave for twenty seconds. A personal addiction, I couldn't begin a workday without this decadent treat.

My lifelong weakness for food intensified exponentially anytime I was out on patrol. For lunch, I frequently craved Kentucky Fried Chicken that I buried in black pepper for maximum taste. I would then wash it down with chocolate milk—one of my personal weaknesses.

Changing of the Guard

On January 3, 1979, I took the oath of the Portage County Sheriff's Office. A new era had officially begun. Getting to work promptly, I met with each shift lieutenant demanding that they adopt a "lead by example" attitude to which they agreed. They were aware that I, too, would lead the same way.

I rotated shift command with the lieutenants one weekend every other month. This gave me an opportunity to work with the squads on the road and provide insight into the deputies' daily concerns. Meanwhile, my wife served as the jail cook and matron and took care of the grocery shopping for the inmates' meals.

Upon taking office, I was slated to earn a graduated salary of about $10,000 less than what the previous sheriff, Nick Check, earned. The Democratic Party of Portage County contested the attempt to pay me less than the man that I just unseated. The result was that I ended up being paid a whopping $1 more.

Equally frustrating was a request from Nick Check that he receive the position of chief deputy, an appointment of the county board. After attending a board meeting prior to taking office it appeared that some of the members were in favor of the request. The chairman asked me how I felt about it. I told him if they insisted on giving Nick that position then they might as well give him my position.

I made requests to the Portage County Board of Supervisors for additional labor and equipment in order to deliver the kind of law enforcement and public protection I believed the people of the county deserved. Unable to procure the financing, I raised the money myself by soliciting donations from local potato growers, most of which had enjoyed a bumper crop the year before.

There were times when some of my supporters would walk into my office to offer a reminder of how hard they worked for me during the election. In return, they wanted me to fix tickets. My reply to them was that I would fix a water leak or perhaps a mechanical problem with a car, but I would not fix tickets. So pay your fine!

Without question, there was a new sheriff in town. Not everyone agreed with my methods of leadership, but I tried my best to provide the type of effective law enforcement that the citizens of Portage County deserved.

8
Sheriff Stories

Law enforcement officers are never 'off duty.'
They are dedicated public servants who are sworn
to protect public safety at any time and place
that the peace is threatened.
—Barbara Boxer

A Real Pain in the Ass

January 8, 1979

During my time as Portage County sheriff, I lived with my family on High-way 54, often referred to as Plover Road, in the Village of Plover. A few days after taking office, I left my house and drove to work in Stevens Point about seven miles away. The road surface was glare ice, a smooth, glassy surface that reflects sunlight. Cautiously, I approached Post Road near the traffic light and came to a stop. I glanced into my rear view mirror and saw a Peterbilt logging truck loaded with pulpwood rapidly sliding toward me from behind. With no time to react, the truck struck my car with such force that it pushed it though the intersection and into a glass telephone booth on the east side of the road. The booth was destroyed and the car suffered repairable damage. When our vehicles came to a stop, the driver stepped out of his truck and ran to my driver's side window. Upset that he had just totaled the new sheriff's squad car, he threw his hands in the air and yelled, "Oh, shit!" Visibly shaken, the man asked me if I was okay. "Except for a sore ass, I'm alright," I replied. The cause of my injury was a spring that had broken and popped through the seat sticking firmly into my butt. Deputy Dick Kostuchowski responded to the scene to give me a ride to my office but not before making a stop at Saint Michael's to have a doctor look at the big bump on my rear end. "You'll be okay," he said after inspecting the injury, "I didn't find any springs in your ass!"

Crafty Cover for a Drug Operation

January 21, 1979

Part of the transition into my new job was acclimation to ongoing criminal investigations. One such happened to be a major drug raid planned by sheriff's detectives and the Drug Investigation Unit of the Wisconsin Department of Justice.

A preceding probe had led officials to Boulder, Colorado, the source of a recent influx of cocaine and heroin into the Badger State. The people who transported the drugs, referred to as "mules," flew on commercial airlines from Colorado to Mosinee Airport (now called Central Wisconsin Airport) and would then drive to the tiny village of Nelsonville at the east end of Portage County for distribution to the central regions of the state.

After offering informants immunity in exchange for the information they provided, we discovered that the Brown brothers, twenty-two-year-old Herman* and his older brother David*—notorious in the area for drug trafficking, had purchased a local assisted living center for senior citizens and were using it to cover their illicit transactions. We also learned that a major shipment of illegal drugs was scheduled to arrive there during the coming weekend. Portage County Judge Robert Jenkins immediately issued a search warrant for the property and we scheduled the bust for the following Saturday to coincide with a farewell party for Nick Check. It would be the perfect date since people would think most of our personnel were attending the event.

Arriving at the senior center at 9 P.M., eight officers and I covered the four entrances of the building. Hearing loud music coming from within, we looked through a window and saw six people who appeared to be in their twenties standing inside. I approached the front door with two state agents and knocked loudly. A man opened the door and then tried to push it closed as we pushed back. I grabbed the man around his chest and he fell back onto a nearby couch with me on top of him. That's when I noticed the pearl grip butt of a large caliber revolver protruding from under the couch, and the man's hand happened to be right next to it. I put my .20 gauge short-barreled shotgun under his neck and ordered him to stay away from it or I would blow his head off. He then surrendered and I handcuffed him. Meanwhile, the two-man team at the side door found it locked so they kicked it in, shocked to find a woman in her late eighties occupying one of the rooms. "You didn't have to kick the door in," said the elderly woman in a soft, faint voice, "I would've opened it for you."

The Brown brothers and their accomplices were arrested and taken to the county jail. But not before David ran to an open safe, grabbed several bags full of heroin, and tried to flush them down a nearby toilet. He was tackled by deputies before he could do so. An ensuing search of the building turned up an abundance of cocaine, heroin, hypodermic needles, and other paraphernalia making it one of the biggest drug busts in the history of Portage County. As the ringleaders of the operation, the Brown brothers were tried in circuit court and sentenced to lengthy terms in state prison.

While incarcerated in the Green Bay Reformatory, David Brown wrote a letter to the editor in the *Stevens Point Journal* stating that the public should be appreciative of the job I was doing as sheriff.

Although the confiscated drugs were traced to Boulder, Colorado, they actually originated in Malaysia. The mules that transported the drugs would fill polyethylene tubes with cocaine and heroin and then push them up their body cavities. According to the Brown brothers, women were much more desirable to get the job done due to their "obvious biological advantage."

Three Hots and a Cot

January 26, 1979

Stevens Point Police reported to Main Street near the market square where a man was trying futilely to break the front window of a clothing store. The officers that responded wrote the man a citation for disorderly conduct and let him go.

The next day my secretary phoned me in my office. "A man I'm not familiar with just walked through the door," she stated. "He's furious and insists on speaking with you personally. What should I tell him?"

"Send him in," I answered.

A man with dirty skin and ragged clothes proceeded to walk through my door. I immediately recognized him as David Disher, a local vagrant with a long rap sheet. "What can I help you with, sir?" I asked.

"I want to talk to you about enforcing the law," he replied with a scowl on his face. "I was in the process of breaking the front window of a downtown department store and the police stopped me. Instead of making an arrest they wrote me a ticket for disorderly conduct." Peering at me through angry eyes, he shouted, "They should've thrown me in jail!"

Because he wasn't, he wanted to press charges against the police department for "not doing their job."

With bloodshot red eyes and slurred speech, David appeared to be under the influence of drugs or alcohol. Hungry and thin, the man was homeless and cold on the city streets. Seeking a warm place to sleep he figured if he committed a crime the local police would make an arrest and take him to jail. There he would have a bed, albeit rudimentary, and three hot meals to eat. Concerned that the man might freeze to death, I instructed the police to bring him to the county jail for the weekend. The officers escorted him upstairs and booked him on a disorderly charge.

While in jail, David was grateful and helpful offering to cook meals and clean the kitchen. On Monday morning, he was released.

Accidental Drowning or Homicide?

Late January 1979

Florian Krutza, a former Portage County sheriff from the 1930s, asked me to look into the old criminal file of a man named Hank Duda. A Portage County sheriff himself in the mid-1950s, Duda went on to become the owner of a drinking establishment called the Platwood Club.

Located on Highway 10 roughly three miles west of Stevens Point on the Wisconsin River, the Platwood Club was as wild as a timber wolf and it howled all night, every night. It was also, at times, lawless. The club, a hive of wanton energy, was a place of thugs and scalawags where harlots, many of which scantily dressed, flirted and giggled with inebriated male customers. Its patrons rode in on Harley-Davidsons, dined on local bratwurst, and chased it down with Point Beer and Pabst Blue Ribbon.

According to witness statements in the Duda file a Platwood Club patron, twenty-seven-year-old Richard Borecki,* had become loud and obnoxious after consuming too much alcohol one night in 1954. As a result, the other patrons began complaining. Duda escorted Richard out of his establishment, took him into an adjacent yard on the river, and returned five minutes later. The following day Richard was reported missing.

The Platwood Club property had a low retainer wall that someone could easily trip over and end up in the Wisconsin River, particularly if under the influence of alcohol. Richard's body was found in the river two days later, recovered by use of a dragline. Observing the man's physical condition, I noticed some bruises on the back of his neck, consistent with a large hand and a strong grip. Bruises on Richard's right wrist were consistent with four thick fingers gripped tightly around it. It appeared that the man might have been grabbed by his wrist with one hand, the back of the neck with the other hand, and flung into the river. Hank Duda, a Golden Gloves heavyweight boxer before becoming sheriff, had a reputation as a bruiser who loved to fight in local bars. At 250 hulking pounds, the man had muscles in places where most people don't have places. Accordingly, many Portage County citizens feared his ability to cause bodily harm to whomever he chose.

I tried to contact some of the people who might have witnessed the incident that night in 1954 but found that some were deceased, some didn't want to talk for fear of retaliation, and others had moved to parts unknown. When I spoke to a circuit court judge, he only confirmed the fact that many people feared Hank Duda. There was no way to reopen the case due to the circumstances. I also spoke to Coroner Bodzislaw who said he shared the same suspicions as Florian Krutza and I, but could find no proof of foul play. Therefore, the death was ruled an accidental drowning.

Fatal Masturbation, a Rancid Body, a Hippie Pathologist, and a Twinkie

March 23, 1979

Twenty-nine-year-old Plover resident Jeffery Helgerson was an employee at the Okray Produce Company, a local potato packing business. Described as quiet and friendly by his neighbors, Jeffery also apparently possessed strange sexual tendencies. On a cold, early spring day, the young man cut the tops off large plastic bags that held 50-pound mesh gunny sacks intended to hold potatoes. He then used them to build a commercial-sized eight-foot-long, four-foot-wide heavy plastic bag. Knowing that cutting off oxygen to the brain can enhance a human orgasm he stripped off all his clothes and crawled inside the bag with a can of Aqua Net hairspray in his hand. He pulled the top of the bag inside twisting the heavy wire around it to make sure it was airtight and then sprayed the Aqua Net to eliminate the internal oxygen. But the man's quest for masturbation-induced pleasure led to accidental suffocation costing him his life.

When Jeffery failed to report for work the following Monday, his supervisor contacted the sheriff's department at about 4:30 P.M. With Deputies Doug Warner and Dick Kostuchowski in tow, I drove to the Zurawski Mobile Home Court to check on the trailer the man was renting. We knocked on the door but there was no response. After obtaining a key from the owner of the trailer, we were able to enter. The heat inside the home was intense and an unyielding stench wafted through the air. Walking into the living room, we found the dead body of Jeffery Helgerson lying face up inside an enormous hermetic plastic bag. With a relaxed smile on his face, the man's right hand still maintained a secure grip on his now flaccid penis.

Jeffery's body had begun accumulating a green slime since it had been sealed inside the bag for nearly three days. The physical form of the man's body was rapidly approaching a state of pure liquid. When the deputies and I cut open the plastic bag to retrieve the decaying body the radiating odor from the buildup of gases was putrid. The fire department placed exhaust fans in the windows to alleviate the stink but they were of little help.

The two deputies placed Jeffery's rotting corpse into an old low-profile ambulance to transport it to University Hospital in Madison. Thankfully for them, the vehicle had half-inch clear Plexiglas installed behind the driver and passenger seats for an impermeable seal. When they arrived, the pathologist, Dr. Robert Huntington, greeted them at the door. Huntington, a tall, longhaired, fully bearded man, often wore hippyish attire that made him appear destitute. But he was one of the most intelligent men I had ever met. The doctor proceeded to inspect Jeffery's body with his two assistants after which they slid it onto a gurney and carried it into an auditorium with bleachers on one side. "Okay, I'll need a couple of witnesses," Huntington said pointing to deputies Warner and Kostuchowski. He then began to open up the cadaver. The deputies said the smell was so intense it made them cross their eyeballs and cover their noses and mouths to keep from vomiting. Dr. Huntington stared talking into a microphone hanging over the body, verbally recording his findings. Suddenly, he reached inside a duffel bag he kept next to his cutting tools and grabbed a Twinkie. He opened the package and took a bite continuing to talk into the microphone with a mouth full of golden sponge cake with creamy filling. The rancid body lying before him with exposed blood and guts didn't bother him one bit. The pathologist then removed the organs from Jeffery's body, weighed them, and recorded the findings with no more than a paper mask over his nose and mouth. Working the cadaver thoroughly, Dr. Huntington was covered with its green slime from head to toe. Some of it had even splashed up onto his face and was dripping from his chin—all while he ate his Twinkie.

To this day, neither Doug Warner nor Dick Kostuchowski will eat or even look at Hostess' most famous snack cake.

Suicide by Locomotive

May 3, 1979

Heading home for dinner late in the afternoon the dispatcher summoned my deputies to a vehicle and train wreck about six miles west of Plover at Rt. 54 and Prairie Drive. The train was traveling east as it approached the crossing while pulling about thirty boxcars. The engineer of the locomotive said as he advanced close a pickup truck stopped on the tracks. He blew his whistle and locked the brakes on the train but the truck didn't move. He could see the driver staring out of his window at the train engine. The train struck the truck broadside and pushed it for more than a quarter mile before coming to a stop. As it did, the truck bounced up and down multiple times on the railroad ties sawing off the top half of the driver's body.

Deputies Art Lepak and Paul Stroik arrived at about the same time. With Art handling traffic I handed Paul rubber gloves and a bag so he could walk the tracks and pick up the man's severed arms and legs. Along with his truck, the man's body had been blown to pieces scattered over a quarter-mile area of countryside. It was imperative to retrieve the body parts so the people who lived in the area wouldn't see them or that animals wouldn't eat them.

Foiled by a Sweater and Corduroys

June 9, 1979

The clock struck 2 P.M. as I sat through mandatory sheriff's training at St.

Norbert's College in Green Bay. Just then, I received a call from Lieutenant Ray Potocki, the commander of our criminal investigation unit in Portage County. He reported what appeared to be a homicide at a residence in the town of Hull just east of Stevens Point. Politely, I excused myself and began the eighty-five mile trek back to the county seat.

Arriving simultaneously to the crime scene, Ray and I saw that the property had been cordoned off with police tape for protection. Investigators had already photographed the interior and the state crime lab forensic unit was en route from Madison. The lieutenant and I walked through most of the house to find its furnishings undisturbed. We then entered the master bedroom to find an elderly woman, possibly in her mid-eighties, lying on the bed with her legs hanging over the side. She had a nylon sock pulled tightly around her neck and a pillow on her face. Her body was stiff to the touch.

Ray and I joined the forensic unit in a search for evidence. There was a beverage glass on the kitchen counter containing a small amount of water and a butter knife lying next to it. A technician lifted the prints from both items. He also lifted prints from the doorknob to the bedroom where we noticed fine scrapes on the latch of the door. It appeared the butter knife was used to slip the door lock. When we entered the basement, we found an open window about sixteen inches high and thirty inches wide that swiveled on hinges. There was an accumulation of fine sand and heavy dust on its concrete sill. Upon closer examination, I found a material print that appeared to be left by corduroy, which I photographed as evidence. As the sun began to set on that side of the house, its rays revealed glistening fibers from a blue sweater made from artificial material. The fibers, caught on the rough metal frame of the window, were also packaged and labeled as evidence.

Two sheriff's detectives went door to door to gather information from neighbors. A middle-aged couple about six houses north of the crime scene said they witnessed a man, perhaps in his late teens, sitting on a bike smoking what seemed to be a marijuana joint. He sat there and stared into thin air for nearly an hour, they claimed, on a jogging trail next to their house. They witnessed the young man wearing a dark stocking cap, a blue sweater, and green corduroys. The next neighbors interviewed by the detectives said they saw the same man and recognized him as the deceased woman's sixteen-year-old nephew, Brian.*

The investigation went late into the night. All those involved met at my office to discuss the collected evidence. We had a strong suspicion as to who may have committed the crime. By this time, it was 2 A.M. on Sunday morning, so we decided that it would be best to wait until daybreak to approach the suspect since he lived at home with his parents.

At 9 A.M. two detectives arrived at Brian's house to fine the young man in the kitchen drying dishes as his mother washed them. They also happened to notice that sitting on top of a hamper against the wall was a neatly folded but soiled blue sweater and a pair of green corduroy trousers. The clothes were confiscated and the sixteen-year-old was placed under arrest for murder.

The young man pleaded not guilty and stood trial. As evidence, the district attorney presented to the jury enlarged photos of the material imprint in the dust as well as the pattern on the corduroys. Crime lab technicians created an overlay that showed a broken cord on the trousers that matched the imprint photograph perfectly. In addition, the material on the sweater was an exact match to the fibers found at the crime scene.

The prosecution explained that Brian was in need of cash to buy drugs and knew that his elderly aunt had some stashed away. The young man went to her house expecting no one to be home. Though the doors to the house were locked, the low-profile window to the basement wasn't latched from the inside. Like a snake, Brian slithered through the opening on his stomach, in the process leaving behind the sweater fiber and the corduroy imprint. He then ascended the steps into the house. Finding that the bedroom where his aunt slept and kept her money was secured, he went into the kitchen and retrieved a butter knife that he used to pick the lock. When Brian opened the door and turned on the light his aunt awoke and sat up in bed. He pushed her back onto the mattress, grabbed a nylon stocking, and wrapped it tightly around her neck until she suffocated. As he ransacked the room looking for money, he noticed his deceased aunt staring straight at him. Bothered by her gaze he laid a pillow on her face so he wouldn't have to see her eyes.

Tried as an adult, Brian lost his case and was sentenced to life in prison.

Juvenile Delinquency

August 15, 1979

I happened to be in the courtroom with Circuit Court Judge James Levi when a boy of about sixteen years of age named Billy* stepped up to the bench accompanied by his mother. The boy had been charged with vandalism and truancy for the second time. If that wasn't enough, the boy's mother insisted on doing all the talking when the judge questioned her son. Judge Levi warned her to keep her mouth shut and let the juvenile answer his questions. But the mother kept interjecting. Finally, the judge decided he had heard enough. "This is the second time Billy has appeared before this bench," he said. "If there's a third time, you're going for a ride, son." He also told his mother that he would find her in contempt of court if she opened her mouth again. "I want you to take that kid home, pull down his pants, and lash his ass," the judge said as he pointed his finger in the mother's direction. "Because if the two of you come back here before me you're both going to jail—the boy for misbehaving, and you for contempt!"

The judge deserved credit for trying to establish some discipline in a household where there appeared to be none. To the best of my knowledge, the boy and his discourteous mother never again appeared in Judge Levi's courtroom.

Attitude Adjustment

September 15, 1979

Deputy Cliff Koziczkowski and I reported to a domestic disturbance call in the Village of Rosholt from Rebecca Barnes,* a woman who was known in Portage County to get around a bit.

When Cliff and I arrived at the address, a small apartment, we found the woman crying profusely. Her makeup was running down her cheeks and her face was swollen showing signs of having been hit. In the apartment were two of the Hazen brothers, Donald* and his younger brother Craig.* Donald was lying on the couch with his feet on the armrest while Craig was pacing the kitchen floor smoking a cigarette. We asked Rebecca the reason for her call. She pointed to a black eye and bruises on her face that she said the man on the couch inflicted. I asked Donald if he struck the woman. "Who the fuck wants to know?" he answered. I asked him to get up from the couch and stand in front of me like a man. "Fuck off, asshole!" he yelled. "Nobody tells me what to do in my own house!" I walked over to the couch and grabbed Donald by the neck. Lifting him up, I threw him against the wall hard enough to crack the plaster and knock several pictures off. "Handcuff his sorry ass," I told Cliff as I acquired the information I needed from Rebecca.

When I finished, I glanced in the direction of Craig who was still pacing the kitchen floor while chain-smoking Marlboro Lights. "Yes, sir" and "No, sir" were the young man's responses to the questions I asked evidently not wanting to suffer the same fate as his brother.

Donald Hazen was charged with disorderly conduct and taken to jail. But the next morning Rebecca withdrew her domestic abuse complaint against him. "I still love Donny with all my heart," she told me.

The man was released after posting bond.

"Prostitution, Pimps, and Perversions"
March 12, 1980

In a small town, certain people command fear based solely on suburban legends. In the case of Hank Duda, however, the legends were mostly true.

A number of Linwood residents contacted me with concerns that the liquor license for Duda's bar, the Platwood Club, was up for renewal. There had been numerous complaints filed by people who lived near the bar about gratuitous nudity or "peddling of flesh" as they liked to put it. The townsfolk asked me to join them in attending a board meeting scheduled for the following Tuesday night at the Linwood Town Hall. Their worry was that Hank Duda would intimidate the board members into renewing his liquor license.

Arriving at 6:30 P.M., I spoke to John Wierzba, one of the town supervisors. He reminded me that Hank could get violent if he heard something he didn't like and that it was a good idea I agreed to attend. John asked me to sit with the board of directors at the front table facing Hank and an intrigued crowd of spectators.

The one-room building, heated by a wood-burning stove, was filled to capacity by the time the meeting started. The town chairman stood from his seat and confirmed that the purpose of the meeting was the liquor license renewal for the Platwood Club. After a brief discussion by the board, the meeting was open to comments. But it seemed that the attendees were afraid to speak up. So I decided to take my turn to talk while Duda sat in the front row with his attorney sneering at me condescendingly. I asked the people to voice their opinions about the bar owner and any incidents they had witnessed at the Platwood Club. "We spoke up against Duda years ago at one of these meetings," said a man near the back of the room, "and then we woke up the next morning to find some of our cattle shot dead." I asked the man if he owned a 12-gauge shotgun. He said that he did. I told him to load it with 00 buckshot and prop it next to his front door. "You have the right to protect yourself, your family, and your property," I told him. I then asked for a show of hands as to how many of the other attendees owned shotguns. Nearly every hand in the room was raised. "I want you to go home and load your guns immediately," I instructed them. "If you don't own buckshot let me know because I have cases of it at the sheriff's department. Are there any more concerns or complaints?"

An elderly lady stood up to voice how she and her family drove to church one Sunday morning and witnessed naked young women walking by the road near the Platwood Club waving to the passing cars. "Prostitution, pimps, and perversions," she said. "That's what Hank Duda is all about." A man spoke up and stated that while he was driving by the club with his family he had to slow down for several motorcycles pulling out of the parking lot with naked women riding on the back waving their hands at the traffic. Others said that when they stopped at the bar for a beer they were harassed and even beaten just for being there. After several other attendees spoke up with their concerns, the open discussion had ended. It was time for the supervisors to vote on the approval or denial of the license renewal. But before the supervisors spoke, I admonished those present for allowing one man to intimidate the entire township, and then strongly urged the town board not to act in Duda's favor.

The vote was unanimous: the bar owner's license was denied. Without hesitation, Duda's attorney announced that they would appeal the board's decision to the circuit court.

After the meeting, John Wierzba invited me to stop for a beer at Vince's Bar where he worked part time. I told him I would be along after I spoke to some of the people leaving the hall. When I arrived at Vince's, Hank Duda walked in shortly after with his two sons. At the time, John was behind the bar and I was the only patron. As I was about to take my first sip of beer Hank began walking toward me. "Let me tell you something, Hintz," he said with a cocksure smile on his face.

"What's that, Duda?"

"When I bust concrete my boys bust concrete," he said implying that his family stuck together no matter what. "When I shovel shit they shovel shit."

"So what are you telling me, Duda? Are you looking for a fight?" I turned to my friend behind the bar. "Hey, John, I think we should dance with this cocky threesome."

Wierzba, a 6-foot-4, 275-pound man, didn't have to think twice. "I'm ready," he said walking out from behind the bar to stand by my side.

Suddenly Duda's expression changed from one of arrogance to modesty. "Look boys," he said, "I didn't come here looking for trouble."

"Then what *did* you come here for, Duda?" I asked.

My question was met with silence and three blank stares.

It became clear that Hank and his sons were trying to scare us. They wanted no part of an actual fight. After cursing under his breath the man turned around and headed for the door, his sons following close behind. Knowing Hank's reputation, I peered out the window into the parking lot to make sure he didn't slash my tires.

The appeal of Hank Duda's liquor license was scheduled in circuit court a few weeks later. Resting comfortably at home with my family on a Friday night, I received a telephone call from Judge Levi. "Does Hank Duda drive a gold Cadillac?" he asked.

"Yes, he does," I replied. "Why do you ask?"

"Well, a gold Cadillac has been circling my block this evening," he said, "and it slows down in front of my house each time it comes around. As far as I can see into the driver's-side window it looks like Hank Duda is the driver."

Hank, it appeared, was trying to intimidate the judge.

"I have a meeting in Milwaukee in the morning," he stated. "Could you check on my wife from time to time since she'll be home alone all day?"

"I'll stake two cars on your house until this whole matter is over," I replied.

There were no incidents at the judge's house and Duda's license denial would be upheld.

One month later, Hank Duda made threats against a Plover man, Bill Adams, at a local tavern. Since it was late at night, I asked Lieutenant Ray Potocki to accompany me and we drove to the scene in unmarked squad cars to not draw attention.

Entering the joint, we walked down a long wooden bar alive with patrons slamming shots of Jezynowka blackberry brandy chased with mugs of frothy Point Beer. Toward the end of the bar we witnessed Bill sitting on a bar stool next to Duda. For the most part, the situation seemed under control. But just in case, Ray stood near the door to keep Duda from fleeing. The former Platwood Club owner motioned for me to walk over and talk to him. "I would enjoy meeting your friend Potocki in the ring," he said with a laugh referring to his experience as a heavyweight boxer. "I could really hurt that boy."

"If you ever lay a hand on my any of my deputies," I told him, "I will hunt you down like a mad dog and blow your fucking head off."

Duda laughed it off and assured me that nothing would happen. But I was certain to keep an eye on him just in case.

An Unusual Hostage Situation

June 16, 1980

The sheriff's department received a complaint from a farmer in Linwood that a herd of twenty-two cattle owned by his neighbor, also a farmer, had broken through a barbed-wire fence and trampled his garden.

Two deputies were dispatched to confront Carl Majkut,* the farmer who owned the cattle. At that instant, Majkut happened to be walking to his neighbor's property to get his stock back. The neighbor, Warren Bronoski,* had surrounded the cattle and locked them in his barn, refusing to give them up. After arguing their respective cases with the deputies, the farmers requested that the "high sheriff" come out to settle the dispute. The deputies called me with the request and I drove to the farm with my statutes book in hand.

Both farmers decided that whatever the statutes called for is what they would agree to. First, I needed to determine who was liable for the fence that the cattle broke through. Wisconsin law stated that a line fence would split accountability for the property. "Each farmer is responsible for the half to his right," said the statutes book. This put the obligation of fence repair on the farmer that owned the cattle. By law, Farmer Bronowski, whose garden was trampled, was entitled to damages at market value of what his plants would have produced. Farmer Majkut, owner of the rambunctious cattle, was required to pay $2 per head to get his herd back and $150 to the neighbor for damage done to the garden and repairs to the fence.

Admittedly, I had no idea there were statutes to address such a dispute;

particularly, the power to hold cattle hostage until justice is served. I also learned that while cattle are detained a farmer has the right to milk them and keep the output.

Unfazed by the Action
July 14, 1980

On this summer Monday afternoon the Portage County Sheriff's Office and Steven's Point Police Department received information that Eric Bird,* a man incarcerated in Arkansas, had escaped and was believed to be headed our way. Bird, who was jailed for armed robbery and drug trafficking, had connections in the Stevens Point area and was expected to contact them for help.

Following the description of a car Bird had stolen, the vehicle was spotted in the parking lot of Shopko, a local retail market. Sure enough, the man was inside the store doing some shopping. Anticipating Bird's return, we surrounded his empty car and waited. Shortly after, an eighty-five-year-old woman exited the store pushing a shopping cart full of groceries. It just so happened that WSPT news reporter Gary Wescott was crouched behind one of our squad cars waiting for the story to unfold. He instructed the woman to duck behind the car because there might be gunfire exchanged, which she did. He then asked her if she knew what was transpiring. "It's probably one of those damn shoplifters again!" she replied wagging her index finger in disapproval. She then climbed into her car and drove away as if nothing was happening.

Without incident, several Stevens Point police officers apprehended Eric Bird as he was walking out of Shopko with groceries in tow. The escapee's car was confiscated and he was held in the county jail until Arkansas officials could transfer him back to their state.

Beer Trailer Accident and a
Surprise under the Car Seat
August 30, 1980

Larry Kleczka,* member of a local Moose Lodge, found himself involved in an unusual accident. Preparing a picnic-style fundraiser for a struggling Portage County family, Larry needed a beer trailer with taps on the outside for beverage service. So he contacted someone from Wausau about thirty miles north who had one to lend. The lodge member then drove there in his pickup truck, hooked the trailer on its hitch, and hauled it back. The road he took, Old Highway 51, was somewhat curvy and rough. After hitting a large bump, the trailer broke loose from the hitch. Bouncing up and down on the highway, it crossed over into the other lane. A few moments later, Larry discovered what was happening and attempted to pull over. At the same time, a Chevy Malibu was rapidly approaching in the other direction and as the trailer bounced up at just the precise time, its wide-angle iron frame smashed through the vehicle's windshield. The impact sheared off the top of the forty-year-old driver's head killing him instantly. When Deputy Dick Kostuchowski and I arrived at the scene, we questioned Larry about the safety measures he took in locking down the trailer. "Hell, Sheriff," he said, "I did everything I could. I even put a padlock through the hitch clip." But when we searched the area for a padlock, we couldn't find one.

The Chevy Malibu was in a shambles of shattered glass, twisted chrome, and mangled metal. Dick and I removed the blood-soaked driver from the vehicle and had him transported to the morgue at Saint Michael's. We then had the wreckage hauled to an impound lot at Tommy Schultz's towing service.

Dick and I felt terrible for the driver of the car being in the wrong place at the wrong time, but we also sympathized with Larry. A large, muscular man, he was crying his eyes out, wondering how something like this could happen when all he was trying to do was help a family in need. He said he took every possible precaution to secure the trailer safely and was driving within the speed limit. Now, not only did he have the death of an innocent citizen on his conscious, he was also likely to face a lawsuit.

A few hours later Dick and I drove back to the office to get started on the obligatory incident reports. I mentioned to the deputy, "You know, the one place we never looked for that padlock was in the victim's car." So I dispatched him to the impound lot to check inside the smashed vehicle. By this time, it was dusk, so he brought a flashlight with him. Climbing inside the front of the car, he leaned over, put his hand under the passenger's seat, and thought he felt something unusual. He pulled his hand out, opened it up, and shined the flashlight only to discover that he was holding one of the victim's eyeballs. By chance, he thought that he had found the padlock because it was cold and hard. When he returned to the office, I could see he was flustered. It was a while before he could eat again.

The padlock was never found.

Drunken Wrestler

September 6, 1980

In the latter part of the evening, the Stevens Point Police Department received a call that things were getting rowdy on the market square. At the dead center of the county seat, the square had about a dozen or so bars where students from the University of Wisconsin-Stevens Point often came to party. When police arrived at the scene, there was a huge crowd of people standing in the road looking upward watching an inebriated man hanging from a streetlight. The man, a wrestler for the university, and rather brawny, had been raising all kinds of hell with the patrons inside one of the bars. After consuming his fair share of alcohol, he went outside, took off his shirt, and stripped his pants down to his underwear. Ascending the metal pole of the nearest streetlight, he slithered out to the arm of the pole and started to do chin-ups about thirty feet above the street, showing off his strength to the people who had gathered below.

When police arrived, the drunken wrestler descended from the light and picked up a beer bottle he had placed next to the base of the pole. He broke the bottle on the sidewalk and used its sharp edges to confront the officers that had formed a circle around the area to keep him from injuring any bystanders.

After hearing the officers' call for assistance, Portage County Sheriff's Deputy Toby Thobaben pulled up in his squad car. There were forty-two law enforcement officers in the sheriff's department at the time whose average size was about 6-foot-3, 230 pounds. Toby, however, was a daunting 6-foot-7, 320 pounds. When he reported to calls, he usually carried a Kel-Lite, a heavy-duty aluminum-bodied flashlight in place of a traditional nightstick. He approached the officers from behind and asked them what the problem was. "Right there is our problem," said one of them as he pointed to the drunken wrestler. "Is that so," Toby stated. In one fell swoop the deputy whacked the wrestler across the head with his flashlight and down he went, knocked out cold. "Is there anything else I can help you guys with?" Toby asked the officers. "If not, I gotta get back on patrol." The crowd of people, mostly UWSP students appalled by the wrestler's behavior, gave the deputy a rousing ovation as he drove away.

A Stevens Point officer put the wrestler's limp body into a squad car and drove him to Saint Michael's where he received twenty stiches for a head wound. He was then booked at the station on a drunk and disorderly charge.

When Toby arrived back at the sheriff's office, he informed me of what happened. "Considering the circumstances," I said, "I think you handled it well."

"There were a bunch of officers just standing around, fully armed," the deputy said, "and they were being held at bay by a guy with a broken beer bottle. So I just reached out and tapped him. End of story."

Airplane Down or
You Do Your Job and I'll Do Mine
October 5, 1980

On a cool, sunny Sunday afternoon, I received a call from dispatch about a single-engine airplane that had gone down in the Wisconsin River. The crash was in the area of a water flowage just west of Stevens Point that powered the local paper mills. The plane, immersed in ten feet of water, was resting next to a small island about one mile west of a boat landing in Bukolt Park. The deputies on duty headed to the sheriff's annex to prepare the rescue boat we used for such emergencies. I met up with them at the park and we were on our way.

When we crossed the flowage to the island, we found the plane upside down with one wing partially above the surface of the water. Scott Rifleman, emergency medical services coordinator with the Stevens Point Fire Department and diver for the Portage County Sheriff's Department, descended into the river to find that the cab of the plane had dug into the silty bottom. He could not see if the pilot was still in the plane.

Four people who were water skiing on the river came to the scene to offer assistance. It was helpful that one of the passengers on their boat happened to be a nurse. With the skiers contributing fifty-foot coils of rope, my thought was to try to pull on the plane's upward-pointing wing to free the cab from the silt. This would afford the diver a chance to check for the pilot. The deputies and I tied one end of the rope to the wing and then attached a second rope with a dog clip, which snapped onto a U-shaped clevis fastener. We wrapped the end of the rope around a tree on the island while one of the deputies pulled the coil tight to take up the slack. The rest of us continued to pull with a ratcheting motion. Our efforts were paying off as the wing began to rise. That is, until the rope broke sending the clevis through the palm of my left hand turning the flesh inside out exposing muscles and tendons. Thankfully, the nurse on the boat had a first aid kit. She carefully washed the wound with peroxide and wrapped it in some clean towels.

A few minutes later, several anglers pulled up to the island saying that the pilot was able to swim to their boat unharmed after which one of them drove him to a nearby hospital. Doctors then examined him and authorized his release. I couldn't help but think that the hard work of the sheriff's department, not to mention my injury, were all for naught.

I stayed at the scene until the job was finished which took about two hours. Deputies Gerald Thrun and Stan Potocki then drove me back to Bukolt Park where a squad car was waiting to take me to the hospital. There, my personal physician, Benivides Palligonis, scrubbed and disinfected my wound and sewed it up with twenty stitches.

The following morning I was back to work with a mitten-like bandage on my left hand. But a few days later, the stitches began to itch. When I took off the bandage to check on my injury, it seemed to have healed, so I decided to remove the stitches myself with fingernail clippers and tweezers. I reapplied the bandages but found that a small area had opened up when I closed my hand. After a trip back to the hospital to see Doctor Palligonis, he steri-stripped the opening and then scolded me when he finished.

"You leave the doctoring to me," he said while poking his index finger in my chest, "and I'll leave the sheriffing to you."

"Fair enough, Doc," I replied, my cheeks bright red with embarrassment.

Election 1980

My first reelection opponent happened to be Al Czech, the cousin of former Sheriff Nick Check (Nick had changed the spelling of his surname some years before), whom I defeated by a three to one margin, again carrying all thirty-nine precincts.

Al's campaign was excessive and expensive due to the fact that Wisconsin business tycoon Norman Meshak pumped a great deal of money into it. Meshak, owner of a multi-million dollar oil corporation, would stop at local bars and buy drinks for everyone present in the name of "Al Czech for sheriff." But it backfired on him when Bill Adams, a friend of mine that owned an excavating company, caught onto what he was doing. Bill would follow Meshak to the bars and buy each patron *two* drinks in the name of "Dan Hintz for sheriff." I later learned that he confronted Meshak with a large wad of cash in his hand and told him, "I'll bet I last longer than you."

Jim Reible, an independent candidate who ran in the election, was sentenced to sixty days in jail in February 1981. A jury convicted him of forging his signature on a $2,170 check at Marathon County Savings and Loan, theft by fraud, and carrying a loaded and concealed .22-caliber pistol.

Dealing with Marijuana

One of my biggest pet peeves as sheriff was the marijuana growing wild in the Almond-Bancroft area of southern Portage County. Not simply because it was unlawful, but because of how it grew in abundance along country roads and in the barnyards of abandoned farms. Cow manure, still plentiful in the area, allowed the "weed" to flourish. Some of the marijuana plants, growing to more than twelve feet tall with three-inch thick stalks, had to be harvested with machetes.

Every few months or so I would join a handful of deputies and drive to the Almond-Bancroft area to cut and harvest the marijuana plants, always using caution since their secreted oil was itchy to the skin. The sheriff's department had an M35 cargo truck, referred to as a "deuce and a half" in U.S. Army terms, that it purchased from military surplus. The deputies and I would fill the truck with marijuana and store it in the annex adjacent to our office. After the weed dried on wooden pallets, I would invite county board members and the news media to a gravel pit in the town of Stockton, and hold a public burn. Doing so made the citizenry was aware that the sheriff's department destroyed the drugs as opposed to having them fall into the wrong hands.

Somewhat jokingly, it was often said that the people living downwind from such public burns got a free high from the resultant plumes of smoke!

Beware the Cowboys

There are good and bad people in every profession and law enforcement is no exception. To that end, it's a fact that some people hate law enforcement officers. Believing otherwise is naïve. Why do they hate? Because some officers are jerks. They're crude, ignorant, pompous, doughnut-consumed, egomaniacs who wear the badge as a justification to harass the public rather than protect it. Thankfully, only a small percentage of officers fall into this category. Anyone with common sense understands that.

✳ ✳ ✳

Experienced law enforcement officers have a good feel for what it takes to be successful in their jobs. That's why I counted on my veterans to help filter out young trainees who weren't exactly "police material."

The Portage County Sheriff's Department would occasionally experience contact with one or more citizens who acted as though they were local police. They always seemed to arrive on the scene at the exact same time as the squad car and they always wanted input, somehow knowing who to suspect. We referred to the individuals as "cowboys."

There were two occasions in 1981 where our department believed we had hired good, honest men to become officers only to realize they were cowboys in disguise. I assigned several of my seasoned officers to ride with the rookies and then turn in reports as to how they acted, talked, and responded when asked questions. The reports would also include what the officers learned about the rookies and what their impressions of them were.

In both cases, the rookies turned out to be problems that I had to terminate immediately, as they were deemed mentally incompetent. One of the rookies, a twenty-three-year-old man, was thought by the officers to be dangerous and unfit to carry a weapon. On his release, a nearby police department hired him. Sure enough, he turned out to be a rogue cop with a penchant for bullying innocent citizens. He even went so far as to fabricate a series of bogus charges against a person simply because he didn't like him. He was fired soon after.

The Portage County Sheriff's Department also faced instances where young men who were picked on when they were in school wanted to become deputies so they could exact revenge on society. My officers knew I wouldn't tolerate jerks who mistreated the public simply because they wore a badge.

Fast Company
October 5, 1981

It was about 8 A.M. as I sipped my early morning coffee at the dispatch center checking the activity logs from the previous night. Suddenly, a call for assistance came in regarding a high-speed car chase.

Beginning about twenty miles to the north in Marathon County, the chase headed south on Highway 51. The pursuers, a Marathon County deputy and a Wisconsin state trooper, apparently got close enough to try to surround the black Camaro they were chasing, but the driver eluded them by swerving onto the wide shoulder and then back onto the road. As the chase approached Stevens Point, roadblocks at the off ramps at Highway 66 and Highway 10 failed to stop the speeding vehicle.

The chase continued past Stevens Point approaching County Trunk Highway B in Plover. With Deputy Jim Grubba using his squad car to block Highway 51 at the CTH B exit ramp, the Camaro began heading west. While the deputy gave pursuit, the chase continued at speeds approaching 100 miles per hour for about two miles. As the two vehicles approached Springville Bridge, Grubba radioed to me that lying just ahead was a school bus in the process of loading children. I asked him if he could move to the left lane to get alongside the Camaro. After replying that he could, I told him to take out the vehicle, which he did by sharply jerking his squad car to the right. As the speeding Camaro spun out it skidded off the road to its right and struck a nearby steel culvert before coming to a rest in the swale of a shallow ditch. The squad car of Deputy Grubba ended up on top of it.

The driver of the Camaro was transported to Saint Michael's with a broken leg and lacerations. Deputy Grubba was fortunate to have suffered only a broken wrist.

Bad Sheriff

May 1982

In law enforcement, it's sometimes tough to set the record straight on contentious issues.

For example, I had four close friends that I used to go fishing with in the Great White North each year. But in 1982, I found myself in trouble for taking my unmarked squad on a seven-day trip coinciding with the Memorial Day weekend.

The squad car, which happened to be a diesel and great on gas mileage, had all my communications equipment, prompting an issue that surfaced during my next reelection campaign. Sure enough, I received several telephone calls on it.

I addressed in such a way that it was my car as sheriff and my form of transportation if I needed to get back to town quickly. It was also my source of communication with my department, which was under order to keep me abreast of what was going on.

A special prosecutor from Wood County hired to look into the matter said he didn't find anything unlawful and that he would issue a press release saying so, which he did—two days after the 1982 election. It didn't matter, however, because I still beat my opponent.

During the same campaign, I was also accused of carrying an illegal weapon—a .20 gauge double-barreled shotgun that I had cut down to fourteen-inch barrels. "Read the statutes," I told my critics, "and you'll discover that I'm well within my power to carry whatever damn weapon I want, including a bazooka if I so choose."

I grew up in a poor but hard-working family that demanded fairness and honesty. If I did something wrong I was punished. If I did something good, I received a pat on the back. When I was a young boy, an old-timer who lived in the countryside once explained to me "a kick in the ass and a pat on the back are only a foot apart. It's all in how you handle it!"

I heeded that statement many times during my law enforcement career. When my political opponents attacked me, I kept my chin up and faced the opposition head on. When I heard rumors that someone was questioning my methods of operating the sheriff's department I would call a press conference and take my message directly to the people, challenging the aggressor to a public debate. Seldom did my detractors take me up on the offer, effectively quashing most rumors.

Election 1982

Detective Gerry Bartkowiak from the sheriff's department ran against me in my second reelection. I invited Gerry to a radio debate during which I made some points that he couldn't counter. The detective, looking uncomfortable and squirming in his seat, couldn't wait to get out of the studio. I could tell from the moment he walked through the door that he didn't want to be there.

Radio host Gary Wescott asked us to keep in mind that we only had two hours in which to debate. Gerry spent most of that time sweating under the collar. "I've attended plenty of forums held by the Democratic Party and listened to many people debate," Wescott told me, "but I admire the way you handle yourself. You're completely comfortable in answering the public's questions."

When our two hours were up Wescott said, "I'd love to have another debate real soon!" Detective Bartkowiak's face was flush with fright as though to say, *We're gonna have a repeat of this? No thanks!*

Afterward, my supporters celebrated the one-sided success of the debate.

In the election, I defeated Detective Bartkowiak handily to maintain my position as Portage County sheriff.

Midday Jailbreak

September 10, 1982

Halfway through the afternoon twenty-six-year-old Jeremy Lesnik* was incarcerated in the Portage County Jail for drug trafficking. About an hour later, his attractive twenty-two-year-old girlfriend Monica* entered the sheriff's department and walked to the top of the stairs standing in front of the metal access door. Though the girl appeared intoxicated, the jailer, Jim Bricusky, let her pass through, perhaps because she had brought a carton of cigarettes for her boyfriend. After handing Jeremy the smokes, she reached into her purse, pulled out a handgun, and pointed it right at Jim. She forced the jailer to unlock the cell and let her boyfriend out. After locking Jim in the cell, the young lovebirds fled in Monica's car.

Suspicion was aroused when a deputy called the jail and received no answer. When he and several colleagues drove to the jail to check on things they went upstairs with their key to the elevator and found no jailer. They yelled Jim's name and heard him yell back from inside one of the cells. He then instructed them as to where the key was to let him out.

Even though Jim was justifiably embarrassed by the incident, I couldn't help but joke with him. "I would have taken the bullet," I told him. "There's no way in hell I would have let some young kid lock me up in my own jail."

Jim just smiled sheepishly.

Later in the evening, Portage County deputies apprehended Jeremy and Monica. The girl, charged with armed jailbreak, was subsequently convicted.

Her boyfriend received a double sentence for his original drug-related crime.

Jim Bricusky, a six-year Stevens Point police officer, had also spent ten years with the Portage County Sheriff's Department. But the embarrassment of this incident affected Jim psychologically to the point where he was compelled to take a medical retirement.

If You Want Something Done,
Do It Yourself
December 8, 1983

Law enforcement officers take risks and suffer inconveniences to protect lives, defend civil liberties, and ensure the safety of fellow citizens. At times, they also endure unusual risks and inconveniences on behalf of the public. Making a difference in the lives of citizens is an opportunity that law enforcement provides that few other professions can match.

For instance, local ambulance service members had gone to the county board in November 1983 to request money for the purchase of new chest thumpers, oxygen tanks, and Scott Air Paks. I was shocked, however, to learn their request was denied due to budget constraints. In response, I decided to raise money for the equipment myself by holding a venison fundraiser. The selling of wild-caught venison is illegal, so I made sure to exhaust all customary financial aid services before going this route. But it proved to be a success since fundraising activities have the lowest involved costs and offer the most impact. I was well aware of the trouble I could face in holding such an event, but in my opinion, the purchase of the emergency equipment was a worthy risk.

(The exchange of venison for money might not sound like a big deal, but the laws prohibiting it help protect America's wildlife ensuring a stable population for future generations. Could you imagine the dramatic decline in deer populations if unscrupulous hunters—as well as those with corporate intentions—were permitted to sell meat from the animals?)

In essence, I wasn't "selling" the venison I was simply giving it away—along with a healthy portion of bear meat—to the fundraiser attendees as a gesture for helping us out in acquiring the equipment. During the previous day, I had commandeered the jail kitchen to pre-cook the meat. Several of my close friends helped with the sides by peeling and preparing one hundred pounds each of potatoes, carrots, and onions. In other words, I offered free venison and bear meat to anyone who purchased a plate of vegetables.

In early December, right after the gun deer season, I would typically hold a "venison feed" where I would invite county judges and local police departments to sample my home-cooked fare for free. I would throw a ton of logs on the grill and, along with Don Gruber, the Wisconsin state game warden assigned to Portage County, would cook until I could no longer stand on my feet. But in this instance, I held the feed at Bukolt Park since it had large fireplaces inside an enclosed shelter—a stone structure built by the Civilian Conservation Corps during World War II. The response to the fundraiser was overwhelming. I placed donation buckets at the front tables where the trays were and the 750 people I fed were happy to donate to an important cause.

About an hour or so into the fundraiser, I looked up from my grill to see six game wardens from the Wisconsin Department of Natural Resources walk through the door. Wearing perfectly pressed gray uniforms they approached me in a rigid procession led by Ron Kobishop, the area supervisor from Wisconsin Rapids. *Oh shit,* I thought, *I'm in big trouble. There are 750 witnesses present to see the DNR haul me off to jail!* With a stern look on his face, I was convinced Ron was going to chew me out for serving the deer and bear meat. "Dan, you son of a bitch!" he howled with a wink and a smile. He and the other wardens walked up to one of the donation buckets and placed a check for several hundred dollars inside. They then grabbed trays and stood at the grill for venison burgers with a side of bear. Along with their vegetables, they devoured their meals in no time flat—seven more happy customers!

By the end of the night the fundraiser concluded without incident and the donation buckets overflowed with more than $3,000, plenty enough to purchase the emergency equipment.

Casket Mystery and Body Exhumation

February-December 1984

When Waldo resident George O'Neal* passed away in February his body was held in a cooler until spring thaw. This way the man could receive a proper burial at Saint Bronislava Catholic Cemetery in Plover in front of family.

On April 30, the man's parents and widowed wife were informed when the body was to arrive and be buried but there was confusion as to the time. When they got to the cemetery, the casket had already been lowered and they were preparing to cover it with dirt. The family was angry that nobody waited for relatives to arrive.

The premature burial also created suspicion.

George's widow, Mary,* believed her husband was buried without a casket. It began when representatives of the Sheboygan Casket Company informed her that the caskets they sold were previously used, relined as if they were rented, not purchased. And a unique bronze casket (the style intended for George) just so happened to arrive at the factory around the same time as the burial. In order to find the truth the exhumation of George's body was necessary. It took me some time, however, to figure out how to accomplish it under such extraordinary circumstances.

First, I spoke to Scott Rifleman who had become the county coroner but he had no idea what to do. Next, I phoned the chief health officer at the University of Wisconsin Hospital in Madison but he also couldn't provide me with an answer. I contacted Judge Robert Jenkins and explained that I needed a writ for exhumation. "Oh my God, Dan" he replied, "the court isn't going to get involved in this type of situation."

* * *

As the warm weather gave way to the cold of winter I decided to drive to Saint Bronislava Catholic Church in Plover to meet with Reverend James J. Logan, explaining to him that I needed to exhume a body suspected of being buried without a casket. The reverend said that since George's body was buried in a Catholic cemetery—sacred ground, as he called it—it was protected by the hand of God. As a God-loving man, I understood what he was saying, but I still had a job to do. For the sake of the law, I begged him to allow me to exhume the body.

"I'm sorry, Sheriff," he said, "but I can't allow you to do it."

"Look, Reverend," I countered, "I was hoping to obtain your permission for this, but I'm going to exhume the body with or without it."

"Well, since you put it that way," he said, shaking his head in disapproval. "I'm still not giving you official permission, but if you're going to do the exhumation I'll ask that you carry it out late at night under the cloak of darkness so it will attract as little attention as possible."

"No problem, Reverend. I'll schedule it for three o'clock in the morning. Would you mind doing me a favor in return?"

"Sure, what would you like?"

"After I'm finished with the exhumation, I'd like you to bless the grave when I close it."

"That, Sheriff, I have no problem doing."

At 3 A.M. on December 12, a representative from the Stevens Point Vault Company arrived at the gravesite with a rack about six feet long and four feet wide and melting torches to help thaw the frozen ground. Together we covered the area with canvass to keep the heat from escaping. Minutes later the ground had softened. We removed the melting torch, dug down about three feet, and hit the lid of the concrete vault. The vault had two big eyebolts to allow the removal of its four-inch-thick cover. With a steel rail and a block and tackle chain, we hooked the eyebolts to a hydraulic lift on wheels that straddled the gravesite. With a flick of the power switch, we expected the lid of the vault to begin its ascent out of the gravesite. Instead, it lifted the entire concrete vault due to its tight seal. We then swung the vault away from the grave hole and used pry bars to open it. I could smell the stench as soon as the vault seal was broken. Pungent and penetrating, it burned my nostrils when I inhaled it. We hadn't thought of wearing any protection such as air-paks or gas masks. "Well, the casket is there," Ray said. Now for the next question: Was George O'Neal's body inside the casket? Ray and I noticed a three-inch deep pool of liquid at the bottom of the vault indicating that it might have drained from the man's body and leaked out of the casket. After opening the casket lid we took some pictures for proof that it was present and George's body was, indeed, inside. The man's shoulders had shriveled to only a few inches wide and he had several dozen grotesque growths on his face that resembled little mushrooms.

At 5 A.M., Ray and I closed the casket and the vault and then walked to the church rectory. Reverend Logan was still awake knowing what we were up to in the cemetery. At about 5:30 A.M. he walked out to the man's grave and blessed it per my request. Ray and I then cleaned up the area the best we could so no one knew we were there.

* * *

Later that day I began to sneeze and my sinuses swelled. For three days, it felt like I had the worst cold ever. Ray experienced the same. The noxious gases from the grave had affected our breathing. When I mentioned it to my doctor, he asked what type of protection I wore at the gravesite. "None," I responded. "You're crazy, Sheriff," he said rolling his eyes in disbelief.

Tornado Outbreak

April 1984

Severe thunderstorms and at least fifteen tornados swept across Wisconsin on April 27, 1984 killing three people and injuring dozens of others.

In Portage County, a tornado was spotted three miles southeast of Stevens Point accompanied by Ping-Pong-ball-sized hail. Two funnel clouds reported in the southeastern part of the county substantially damaged a barn and two homes. At one of the homes, the storm destroyed a garage, crushed two cars, tore off the roof, and blew out the windows.

A friend of mine, Pete Kopeko, owned a 500-acre deer farm in the area, 400 acres of which was densely wooded white oak. An F-2 a tornado cut through the center of it damaging so many trees that he was able to log the residual lumber and use it to build a four-bedroom home with a pole shed in Stevens Point.

Ethan Waskiewicz* and his cousin Matthew* owned farms about a quarter mile apart on opposite sides of Highway 51, both of which were struck by the same tornado. A twelve-inch square beam about thirty feet long was carried by the high winds east to west across the highway. It was then driven like an arrow through Ethan's humble farmhouse causing it to protrude from both ends.

At Matthew's farm there was a sizable bunk feeder—a metal trough on wheels about fifty feet long where cattle could eat from both sides. The tornado lifted the feeder off the ground and spun it around several times to where it sheared off the top half of a concrete silo. By the time the feeder hit the ground, it was twisted like a pretzel. The numerous tops of the red oak trees that grew around Matthew's barn were also sheared off. Yet the tornado didn't touch but one shingle on the farmer's house.

The death and injury toll from the storms, which struck on a Friday afternoon, could have been much worse. Had the storms arrived one day later when travelers and seasonal tourists were unwinding in the affected areas it might have proved catastrophic. Thankfully, there were no deaths in Portage County.

The tornadoes brought back memories of when I was young. In the mid-fifties, my father drove my brothers and me several miles from our farm to view property damage that occurred from an F-3 tornado. One of the worst tornadoes to that point in Wisconsin history, it destroyed most of a neighboring farm. It lifted a fifteen-foot-high barn into the air before smashing it to the ground. A cow was standing contentedly on the roof of the barn eating hay. The tornado also tore patches of hide off most of the dairy cows. The wind velocity of the storm twisted brass beds from the farmhouse like corkscrews and drove strands of hay through an oak tree about four inches thick.

The Unsolved Murder of Janet Raasch

October-November 1984

Like so many others who have worked in law enforcement, I am haunted by unresolved cases. One particular case—the murder of Janet Raasch, a twenty-year-old University of Wisconsin-Stevens Point student—continues to weigh heavily on my mind.

A business major in her third year at UWSP, Janet lived on campus in Watson Hall and worked at the nearby DeBot Dining Center. On or near October 11, she had switched shifts with a fellow student so that she could travel home to Merrill, a town about forty-nine miles to the north on Highway 51. The young woman's mother had died from cancer several days before and she wanted to spend time with her family. A male acquaintance and several UWSP students told Portage County law enforcement officials that they dropped Janet off near an intersection on State Highway 54 on October 11.

That was the last time she was seen alive. Her friends then reported her missing four days later.

On November 17, deer hunters discovered Janet Raasch's partially clothed and badly decomposed body about 300 feet into a wooded area south of Stevens Point in the town of Buena Vista near the intersection of Highway 54 and County Trunk J.

An autopsy performed by Dr. Robert Huntington in Madison revealed nothing conclusive, but the forensic pathologist did say that Janet appeared to have been strangled. He also suggested that due to the bodily decomposition she appeared to have been dead in the woods for ten to twelve days as opposed to the thirty-five days between her disappearance and the day she was found. The doctor and I agreed that the decomposition of the body happened over this time frame and then stopped when the chill of the Wisconsin autumn began to preserve the body.

A suspect in Janet's murder lived in a small cabin converted from a church rectory on County Trunk Highway JJ (CTH JJ) about a half-mile northeast of State Highway 54. When Portage County Sheriff's Detectives Pete Thrun and Leroy Doescher went to the cabin to question the reclusive man, he offered few details. But he did acknowledge picking Janet up in his car in Plover and that he gave her a ride to the intersection of Highway 54 and CTH JJ. He said he dropped her off there and then turned up the county trunk heading home never to see her again. The suspect's admission implied that he and Janet might have been acquaintances. But why he would have given the young woman a ride remains unclear. By itself, the suspect's account wasn't incriminating enough to arrest him. A few months later, however, the man moved to Illinois. I dispatched several detectives to try to locate him and question him further but his exact whereabouts in the state couldn't be pinpointed.

Many questions remain in the Janet Raasch murder case. For instance, if the young woman was given a ride to Merrill, north of Stevens Point, why would she be hitchhiking south past Highway 51, the only highway that leads to

Merrill? On Highway 54, which runs east to west, she was at least two miles past 51. If she was able to get a ride from someone who apparently was only willing to go as far as the intersection of Highway 54 why didn't she get off at the intersection of Highways 54 and 51 and then hitchhike to Merrill from there? But then if she got a ride from friends why would she be hitchhiking in the first place?

The fact that several UWSP students drove Janet south even though she ended up hitchhiking in the opposite direction to Merrill made them suspects. But when officials questioned them about their peer's disappearance, the answers they offered didn't raise any suspicions. Those same students also revealed that Janet had friends in Green Bay. Since Highway 54 goes to Green Bay, there was speculation that she might have changed her mind about visiting family and instead decided to visit her friends. It also happened that the reclusive suspect lived on CTH JJ just off Highway 54 about a half-mile or so.

Since Janet's murder in the fall of 1984, investigators have followed a number of leads, some extending as far as Maryland and Pennsylvania, but they have been unable to make an arrest in the case. In 2002, the Wisconsin Department of Justice exhumed Janet's body from St. Paul Lutheran Cemetery in Marathon County to perform DNA testing. The Raasch family held out hope that modern forensic technology would lead to evidence and a conviction, but it never did.

In the summer of 2013, Janet's unsolved murder was among several cases profiled by Gannett Wisconsin Media during a month-long newsprint series. Soon after, law enforcement officials with the Portage County Sheriff's Department acknowledged that the media coverage prompted someone to write an anonymous letter that might hold some clues in identifying the young woman's killer. County officials have urged the person to come forward believing he or she may be withholding additional details about the mysterious death.

* * *

While the unsolved murder of Janet Raasch is more than three decades old, the case hasn't gone cold. As of this writing, the Portage County Sheriff's Department continues to look at a number of possible leads and suspects.

The Raasch family, tormented by dead ends, sorrow, and frustration, remains in touch with investigators hoping that one day they will inform them that the case of Janet's murder has been solved.

Anyone with information about this case is encouraged to call the Portage County Crime Stoppers Hotline at 1-888-346-6600 or contact the Portage County Sheriff's Department at (715) 346-1400 or sheriff@co.portage.wi.us. Anonymity is guaranteed.

Getting Away with Murder?

July 14, 1985

The tiny Village of Iola on Highway 61 is known not only for its infamous rock festival but also for its pristine country setting. In the early 1980s, it had a small full-time police force consisting mostly of Police Chief Michael Schertz and his one full-time officer, Gerald Mork.

Schertz, with his abrasive personality, was more tolerated than liked by the public he served. He had garnered a reputation that complemented his appearance: full-sized and fierce, with a penchant for enforcing laws strongly. Mork, on the other hand, was known as a soft-spoken man who preferred to address issues through listening and observation as opposed to forced compliance. The subsequent friction that existed between the fourteen-year police chief and his young officer of eight months was no secret among the citizens of Iola.

The son of Waupaca County Sheriff William Mork, Gerald seemed to be favored as an up-and-coming law enforcement officer by some of the local board of directors, which infuriated Schertz. The police chief repeatedly attempted to have the young man dismissed and had expressed frustration with the board members' refusal to cooperate in disciplining him. Schertz claimed that Mork was insubordinate, had misused his firearm and squad car, and once stole two confiscated twelve-packs of beer.

During the Iola Car Show of July 14, 1985, Chief Schertz and Officer Mork patrolled the village in separate squad cars. As evening fell, the officer received a radio message from his boss demanding that he meet him at the local cemetery located three blocks from Main Street. "I saw the lights of the officer's squad car among the gravestones," said an elderly man sitting on a bench at the corner of Main Street and Cemetery Road, "then he was followed by the chief's car about one minute later. Before long, I heard two sounds that sounded like gunfire." Afterward, the man said he saw the chief's car come from the direction of the cemetery and gradually turn right onto Main Street. A passerby happened to witness a squad car parked in the cemetery near the entrance with its driver's-side door open, but no lights on. When he pulled up to the vehicle, he noticed something on the ground. He got out to investigate and witnessed Officer Mork lying face down on the ground in a pool of blood, shot twice in the back of the head with a .38-caliber semi-automatic pistol. He called 911 and reported it to the Waupaca County Sheriff's Department, which dispatched a squad car.

Officer Mork's revolver, still in its holster, was strapped shut. The young man had not radioed in his location and it remains unclear as to why he stepped out of his squad car at the cemetery.

Regardless, it didn't take long for his father to determine a suspect with a motive.

On July 25, 1985, Waupaca County Sheriff William Mork dispatched his deputies to the home of Michael Schertz who immediately took the Iola police chief into custody and charged him with first-degree murder.

I received a phone call from Sheriff Mork later that night with a request for a special favor. He asked if I would hold Chief Schertz in one of my prison cells to sidestep any controversy since the murder victim happened to be his son. I agreed to hold the suspect in the Portage County Jail until his arraignment several days later.

The trial that followed was shocking.

* * *

The attorneys for Michael Schertz filed for a change of venue resulting in the trial being held in Fond du Lac County. The defense built its case on the fact that the weapon used to shoot Officer Mork, a .38-caliber handgun, was missing from the evidence locker at the police station. A statement filed by Waupaca County police with Schertz's arrest warrant confirmed that the bullets and shell casings found at the scene were .38-caliber, possibly from a Baretta automatic pistol. Schertz admitted confiscating such a weapon from a county citizen in 1982, but claimed to have destroyed it. He then changed his story and said he sold it to two men he had met in a bar in another county for $100 because he was desperate for cash. He said he did not know who the men were and hadn't seen them inside or out of the bar since.

In one of the most startling revelations in the case, a part-time Iola police officer told investigators that Chief Schertz said he was contemplating slitting Officer Mork's throat. Waupaca County residents often knew Schertz to use excessive force in making arrests, but no allegations were serious enough to require action. If Mork had any reason to fear Schertz, he did not speak of it to anyone.

Although the case seemed to point to Michael Schertz's guilt, a jury acquitted the police chief based on insufficient evidence and the fact that there were no witnesses to the shooting. Schertz was later charged with the theft and sale of his .38-caliber gun. He had been suspended from his position at the onset of the murder investigation, but later resigned. The former police chief then moved from the state of Wisconsin to whereabouts unknown never to be seen or heard from again.

Officer Gerald Mork, who also served as fire chief for the Village of Iola, was survived by his wife, a six-year-old daughter, and a two-year-old son.

November 1970: The first group to graduate from the North Central Technical Institute in Wausau, Wisconsin for Law Enforcement Officer Certification. Three of the four attendees from Portage County went on to serve as sheriff. That's me in the second row from bottom, third from left. I served four terms from 1979-1987. Tom Wanta, second row from top, far left, served two terms from 1987-1991. Peter Thrun, third row from top, second from right, served one term from 1993-1995.

As a sheriff's deputy in December 1972 booking an inmate into the Portage County Jail on charges of cocaine possession

June 15. 1975:
Posing with a
Beatles-esque haircut
in my office in the
basement of Village Hall
during my first week as
Plover police chief.

Artist Sidney G.
Rzentkowski's
rendition of the
Plover police chief
in 1975.

THE POINTER

September 28, 1978   Vol. No. 8

THE LAW AND DAN HINTZ

off-campus price: 15 cents

September 1978: *The Pointer* is published by the University of Wisconsin—Stevens Point. While sheriff, I received a great deal of elective support from the school and many of its students.

September 1978: "I'm not more conservative, just more concerned."

July 1978: Cruising the Plover Parade with my wife Shirley in a Ford convertible owned by Dorr and Irene O'Brien—two of my best supporters. We usually walked the parades and handed out campaign literature. but on a hot summer day, we took the easy way out.

The trophy-winning Shantytown Bionic Polacks rope pull team in the summer of 1978. Top row left to right: Beverly Stanczyk, Tony Dombrowski, Terry Firkus. Joe Wierzba, Billy Wanta, Dan Hintz. Norbert Wierzba. Chet Stanczyk. Bottom row: Jim Wierzba, Jerry Wierzba, Stan Lemke, Don "Butch" Kirsling, Gene "GG" Walczak. (Not pictured: Arlen Tuskowski)

WANTED!
DAN HINTZ
⟩⟩ DEMOCRAT ⟩⟩
for Portage County Sheriff.

- OVER 10 YRS. LAW ENFORCEMENT EXPERIENCE - CHIEF OF POLICE SINCE 1975.
- MARRIED 14 YEARS • FATHER OF THREE • EXPERIENCED • HONEST • EFFECTIVE • ARMY VET
- LIONS CLUB • HOLY NAME SOCIETY MEMBER • LAY MINISTER — ST. BRONISLAVA'S CATHOLIC CHURCH
- SEC.-TREAS. NORTH CENTRAL POLICE CHIEFS ASSOCIATION • EX-OFFICIO - PUBLIC SAFETY COMMITTEE

REWARD!

The best possible Public Law Enforcement Services your money can buy. Good Communications with Local and Out Lying Communities. Good Solid Control of Spending your Tax Dollars. Sound Attack and Control of Drug Traffic and an Educational Program for our Youth.

☞ VOTE - Hintz Democrat for Sheriff - Sept. 12.

This imaginative campaign poster was created by Mark Colrud, a former Plover police officer. It garnered a lot of attention from the people of Portage County in the summer of 1978.

One of my prized possessions. Shirley special-ordered this amethyst ring after I won my first election for sheriff in 1978. I still wear it daily.

The infamous "Buford" stick—twenty-one and a half inches of solid maple

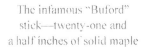

A personalized handmade leather holster presented to me by the Wisconsin Sheriffs' and Deputy Sheriffs' Association. I wore it on the job without fail every day that I was sheriff. It held a Smith and Wesson .357 Magnum with a three inch barrel—a lethal piece loaded with 158-grain semi-jacketed. hollow-point bullets.

Sworn in for my first term as sheriff in January 1979
with County Clerk Roger Wrycza

January 3, 1979: My first day in office as sheriff of Portage County,
proud to lead one of the best departments of men in the state of Wisconsin

January 1979: The first Portage County Sheriff's Department group photo from my initial term in office. Four of the individuals pictured were elected county sheriff after I left office in 1987: Tom Wanta, fourth row from bottom, far left, served from 1988-1991; Ron Borski, fourth row from bottom, far right, served from 1992-1994; Stan Potocki, first row, second from left, served from 1998-2002; John Charewicz, top row, far right, serving from 2002-present. Missing from the photo is Pete Thrun, sheriff from 1995-1997.

Media photo taken during my first term
as Portage County sheriff

February 1979: Marijuana, hash, and drug paraphernalia confiscated during a drug bust at a residence in the town of New Hope. Estimated street value of the drugs was $8,000-$10,000.

Marathon County Sheriff Louis Gionoli asked me to walk with President Jimmy Carter to provide him with some additional security as he greeted supporters at the Central Wisconsin Airport in March 1979

July 28, 1980: A media interview while roughly 8,000 marijuana plants worth about $13,000 burned in a gravel pit in the town of Stockton. I chose to conduct public burns of illegal drugs so the public could witness how the Portage County Sheriff's Department confiscated illegal contraband and avoid any suspicions as to what happened to the drugs after the cases were closed. There were rumors that the homes downwind of this bonfire enjoyed a "cheap high" during the burn.

October 8, 1981: After soaking this illegal stash of marijuana with gasoline and fuel oil, I wrapped a rag around the end of a thin strip of wood and lit it on fire. I threw the strip into the marijuana while Frank Barbers, chairman of the Portage County Law Enforcement Committee, stood next to the vehicle in the photo. The cap that Frank was wearing flew off his head when the drugs ignited.

RE-ELECT DAN HINTZ
SHERIFF TUESDAY, SEPT. 9

This primary election is the most important for the Portage County Sheriff race. Your choice is TOMORROW, SEPTEMBER 9.

VOTE DAN HINTZ SHERIFF
TUESDAY, SEPT. 9

The following additional people support Dan Hintz for Sheriff

Rodney Houk
Loretta Houk
Bill Jurgella
Florence Jurgella
Carl Wohlbier
Kay Wohlbier
Joe Jurgella
Mary Jurgella
Jim Treder
Louise Treder
Erv Rakowski
Ruth Rakowski
Richard Jurgella
Marilyn Jurgella
John Pezewski
Pat Pezewski
Lawrence Wolosek
Mary Nowak
John A. Prutz
LeRoy C. Feltz
Joan Feltz
Joyce Stroik
Francis J. Miloch
Chet Wolosek

Jerry Hintz
Joe Kruzitski
Anita Kruzitski
Lawrence Groholski
Nicholas L. Meronek
Vicky Meronek
Mark Meronek
Michael Meronek
Matt Meronek
Jerry Meronek
Sandra Meronek
Johana Mansavage
Lawrence Mansavage
Joe Alfuth
Larry Slusarski
Bruce Dehlinger
Bob Milanowski
Clifford Bembenek
Pauline Bembenek
Fred Schultz
Gerald Brandt
Alvonne Brandt
George Wherritt
Jane Wherritt
Wally "Spaatz" Wisa

A support advertisement published in the *Stevens Point Journal* during my reelection campaign in 1980. The individuals listed contributed $2 to have their names appear, which paid for the cost of the advertisement.

June 21, 1984: Shawano County Sheriff James Knope and I address
the national media about the removal of the terrorist group Posse Comitatus.

November 12, 1986: Taken at an auto auction and memorabilia show in Wausau, this photo includes two of the greatest professional athletes of all time. On the left, the "Golden Boy," Paul Hornung, Pro Football Hall of Famer and one of my favorite Green Bay Packers. On the right, Pete Rose, seventeen-time Major League Baseball All-Star. Nobody played America's pastime quite like "Charlie Hustle." The National Baseball Hall of Fame should have inducted him years ago.

With son Kevin at Raymond James Stadium in Tampa for Packers vs. Buccaneers on November 24, 2002

Proud to be a lifelong Packers fan!

This is what was left of the Hintz family farmhouse after a fire in 2007. The property was purchased by local interests soon after and the burnt remains were leveled. The house may have been lost, but its memories remain.

Summer 2014: The Hintz family in
Treasure Island, Florida

9

OPERATION CLEAN SWEEP: REMOVAL OF THE POSSE COMITATUS

*The only thing necessary for the triumph of evil
is for good men to do nothing.*
—Edmund Burke

In the 1970s and 1980s, a farm crisis in the American heartland coupled with rising unemployment spurred the growth of several right-wing survivalist groups, particularly across rural areas of the nation. One of those groups, the Posse Comitatus (pah-see coh-mitt-tah-tus) was one of the most investigated in American history.

To understand what occurred between the Posse Comitatus and me during my time as sheriff of Portage County, and why I acted to remove them, it is useful to know who the group is, where it came from, and the enduring threat it posed.

Jewish Money Barons, Mud People, Satanic Offspring, and the Ku Klux Klan: A Brief History of the Posse Comitatus

Strictly translated, the term posse comitatus is Latin for "the ability of the county." Through the years, it has taken on such loose definitions as "power of the county," "power of the citizenry," or "possible force." Historically, the term originates from the Posse Comitatus Act: a United States federal law signed on June 18, 1878 by President Rutherford B. Hayes. The purpose of the act, in conjunction with the Insurrection Act of 1807, is to limit the powers of the federal government in using the military to act as domestic law enforcement personnel. It was passed as an amendment to an army appropriation bill following the end of Reconstruction, and was subsequently updated in 1956 and 1981.

* * *

Posse Comitatus also happened to be the name chosen by a right-wing, anti-tax extremist group established in 1969 in Portland, Oregon. The founder of the group, Henry Lamont Beach, was a retired dry cleaner and one-time member of the Silver Shirts; a Nazi-inspired organization conceived in the United States after Adolf Hitler rose to power in Germany in 1933.

Although Beach founded the Posse Comitatus, much of the group's history can be traced back to Arthur Porth of Wichita, Kansas. Porth, a building contractor, argued that the 16th Amendment was unconstitutional since it placed taxpayers in a position of involuntary servitude contrary to the 13th Amendment. Porth was convicted on numerous tax evasion charges and became a grass-roots hero to the emerging tax protest movement of the late 1960s. Retired Colonel William Potter Gale, who helped coordinate guerrilla resistance in the Philippines during World War II, eventually took over the Posse from Beach.

While in prison, Arthur Porth received the support of several other far-right individuals, many of whom tied their racist views into his anti-tax protests. In 1967, one of those individuals, Martin A. Larson, wrote in an article for the right-wing extremist periodical *American Mercury,* "The negroes in the United States are increasing at a rate at least twice as great as the rest of the population." He warned that the tax burden posed by blacks "unquestionably doomed...the American way of life." Larson later wrote regular columns for the white supremacist magazine *The Spotlight.* In them, he often referred to black women as prostitutes whose "offspring run wild in the streets, free to forage their food in garbage cans, and grow up to become permanent reliefers, criminals, rioters, looters, and, in turn, breeders of huge litters of additional human beings to the same category."

The Posse Comitatus functioned on the belief that the true intent of the founders of the United States was to create a Christian republic where the citizen is sovereign. Members of the group believed the federal government was illegitimate, operated by Jewish money barons through the Internal Revenue Service, the Federal Reserve, and the federal court system. The Posse had strong ties to the white supremacist Christian Identity movement whose members believed they were the true Israelites chosen by God. The Jews, they claimed, sought to help Satan destroy civilization.

The Posse's modus operandi comprised vigilante law enforcement, tax protests, counterfeiting, murder, terrorism, illegal arms sales and stockpiling, and paramilitary training; all of which were viewed as politically necessary, lawfully justified, and, according to Christian Identity, sanctioned by God.

Believing that the collapse of society was imminent, the Posse collected weapons and conducted field exercises in armed self-defense and reconnaissance. The group's members stockpiled large quantities of grains, dried foods, canned goods, water, and vitamins in anticipation of long-projected economic or political collapse and racial rioting.

In the 1940s, former Methodist minister Wesley Swift, a hero of the Posse Comitatus, had deep ties to several radical right-wing groups including the Ku Klux Klan. Swift and his accomplices integrated Christian Identity principles into a loosely organized racist and anti-Semitic belief system. The former minister argued that only the white race was created in the form of God while African and Asian races, produced from the "beasts of the field," were subhuman creations. Swift also maintained his own personal version of the biblical Book of Genesis in which Eve—the wife of the first "true" man, Adam—was seduced by the evil Serpent who pretended to be a white man. Eve then bore a son, Cain, who was the actual father of the Jewish people. This elucidation, often referred to as the "two-seed" theory, supported the propensity of the Posse Comitatus to demonize Jews, whom the group often acknowledged as the "spawn of Satan." Some Posse proponents also claimed that subhuman races have existed before the biblical presence of Adam and have spawned the non-white races of the world, which they labeled as "mud people."

The Racist, Anti-Semitic Salesman

In the mid-1970s, Jim Wickstrom, a tool salesman and former mill worker, saw what he believed to be less-qualified black workers bypassing him in receiving raises and promotions. They were getting ahead, according to Wickstrom, simply because they were black, and that enraged him. It also compelled him to follow in the footsteps of Henry Lamont Beach, Arthur Porth, and William Potter Gale in becoming an adherent of Christian Identity ideology and a member of the Posse Comitatus.

By the late 1970s, Wickstrom had moved back to his childhood state of Wisconsin from his home in Missouri at the invitation of Don Minniecheske, a businessman who owned 570 acres of land on the shores of the Embarrass River. It was Minniecheske's intent to create a "township" for the Posse that would operate without recognition of federal, state, or local laws and he wanted Wickstrom to be part of it. After building a tavern and moving several trailers onto the land—located in Shawano County about forty miles northeast of Stevens Point—the two men named the property The Constitutional Township of Tigerton Dells. They then posted signs that said, "Federal Agents Keep Out, Survivors Will Be Prosecuted." Wickstrom named himself the township's judge and municipal clerk and began traveling the Midwest farm belt, appearing at town meetings, agriculture shows, entertainment venues, and in the living rooms and basements of homes in an attempt to recruit more Posse members.

Apparently, the efforts of Wickstrom and other recruiters were paying off. By 1979, the FBI estimated that the Posse Comitatus had seventy-eight chapters in twenty-three states with more than 50,000 members mostly in the upper Midwest and the Great Plains states.

Jim Wickstrom had long been a thorn in the side of central Wisconsin law enforcement. He frequently advocated the mass murder of Jews, non-European Americans, homosexuals, drug addicts, and race traitors in accordance with the Christian Identity movement. He and other armed members of the Posse Comitatus often blocked a public road that ran past the group's compound for the purpose of keeping outsiders away from Tigerton Dells. Also, the Posse had been cited for zoning law violations since the land on which their mobile homes were parked was not residentially zoned. When several central Wisconsin sheriffs served papers to Wickstrom ordering the removal of the trailers from the property, he refused. The Posse leader was also mailed a certified letter ordering his group's members to stop firing weapons at their shooting range inside the compound because they were disturbing the citizens that lived nearby. "If you want our guns," Wickstrom replied, "come and take them."

The Posse Comitatus received widespread media attention in February 1983 when another leader of the group, Gordon Kahl, was involved in a violent standoff with law enforcement officials near Wounded Knee, South Dakota. Convicted for failure to pay taxes and then subsequent violation of his probation, Kahl shot and killed a U.S. marshal and deputy marshal who had attempted to arrest him. As the national media reported on the fatal confrontation, CBS news anchor Dan Rather went a little further than most of his associates labeling Kahl as "a fanatic and an ultra-right-wing tax protestor." Federal law enforcement officials, however, called him a killer.

Shortly after, Jim Wickstrom appeared on the nationally televised *Phil Donohue Show*. The host asked Wickstrom about the murder of the two officials at the hands of Gordon Kahl, but the Posse member quickly changed the subject arguing that Kahl's civil rights were violated. He claimed that the real issues at hand were corrupt courts, farm foreclosures, the Federal Reserve, foreign workers, income tax, and Jews. Four months later, Kahl died in a bloody standoff with law enforcement in Arkansas making him a martyr to the Posse Comitatus. Kahl's death also accelerated the terrorist group's expansion.

In summer 1984, Wickstrom was imprisoned for operating an unlawful guerrilla training camp at the Posse's Tigerton Dells community, but was able to escape from federal custody. He was recaptured later in the year, but not before promising that the Posse's foes, particularly federal agents and Jews, were about to face "the biggest bloodbath you can imagine." That bloodbath, however, never occurred. Wickstrom would spend a year in prison, see his Tigerton Dells community seized, and many of his group's members arrested. Subsequently, the former salesman would spend three more years in jail for counterfeiting and illegal firearms possession. Upon his eventual release, he became a popular speaker at neo-Nazi functions where he would often tell attendees, "I live for the day I can see heads on fence posts," presumably referring to those of Jews and minorities.

Jim Wickstrom maintained a tremendous influence over other members of the Posse Comitatus. For instance, in the summer of 1985, Michael Ryan, the leader of the Nebraska Posse Comitatus branch, and his fifteen-year-old son Dennis, tortured and killed a man. For three years, Michael had followed the teachings of Wickstrom who told him to prepare for Armageddon in the form of a race war—whites versus blacks and Jews.

Wickstrom had adopted Dennis as somewhat of a protégé, making him a leader in local Posse circles. Later in 1985, Dennis, on the orders of his father and possibly Wickstrom, shot twenty-six-year-old Posse member James Thimm in the face after Thimm angered some of his peers. When Thimm survived the shooting, Michael chained him inside a hog shed, kicked and beat him, and forced him to have sex with a goat. Dennis then shot off Thimm's fingers and partially skinned him. The elder Ryan sodomized Thimm with a shovel and finally beat him to death, the entire ordeal lasting approximately two weeks. Dennis would serve a twelve-year prison sentence for his role in James Thimm's death.

Toward the end of 1985, Michael Ryan became obsessed with religion and his belief that racial Armageddon was imminent. He became increasingly violent turning his attention to Luke Stice, the five-year-old son of Posse Comitatus member Rick Stice. Ryan declared the child a spawn of Satan and convinced the boy's father to help inflict unspeakable physical and sexual abuse upon him. The boy survived until spring, when Ryan broke his neck in a fit of rage. Rick Stice helped bury his own son.

For his crime, Michael Ryan was sentenced to death. Some thirty years after the murder of Luke Stice, the former Posse Comitatus member remains on death row at the Tecumseh State Correctional Institution in Nebraska. In 2013, Ryan's lawyer sought unsuccessfully to have his client's sentence overturned.

The Terrorists Next Door

After more than ten years of expansion, the Posse Comitatus mobilized and gained national attention. In the early 1980s, the group became a substantial, and feared, political movement.

Posse members headquartered in Tigerton Dells frequently disrupted local government assemblies, threatening and assaulting public officials. One of the first and most significant examples was a 1975 death threat made by the Posse against Vice President Nelson Rockefeller. By the start of the farm crisis, such violent threats and acts only increased.

In 1982, police discovered that seven Posse members were plotting to murder several federal judges and blow up an IRS operations center in Denver, Colorado.

*   *   *

There was also a manual ostensibly written by Posse Comitatus leaders that called for members to engage in terrorism and prepare for guerrilla warfare. The manual purportedly instructed the Posse to "seek out its enemies" and "fight 'em, blow them apart with gunfire, cannons, mortars, rockets, mines, flame throwers, booby traps, whatever you can muster. Pound them down into the rubble." It also stated that guerrilla warfare was "a war of attrition" that could "bring people together against those in power, connected with economic, racial, ethnic, and social issues." Jim Wickstrom reportedly used the manual for recruiting purposes and during the Posse's paramilitary training in the early 1980s.

A previous Posse Comitatus manual published by Henry Lamont Beach in the 1970s allegedly stated, "Officials of government who commit criminal acts or who violate their oath of office…shall be removed by the Posse to the most populated intersection of streets in the township and, at high noon, be hung by the neck, the body remaining until sundown as an example to those who would subvert the law."

Due to such beliefs, violence was expected as central Wisconsin law enforcement officials sought to remove the Posse Comitatus from its Tigerton Dells property.

How it Began: A Traffic Stop, a Meeting with the Governor, and Basic Surveillance

In November 1981, I was elected northeast area director of mutual aid by the sheriffs and chiefs of police of the state of Wisconsin. The mutual aid system was established to deal with state emergencies that required a mass of law enforcement personnel. The system functioned solely with the support of the governor, as it required the state to reimburse the county that suffered the disaster for all costs of law enforcement and other emergency responders.

The responsibility of the mutual aid director was to order and coordinate the level of assistance required to handle each emergency. Each county sheriff had a copy of the procedural manual, which dictated the response of each county. The sheriff would serve as assistant coordinator and utilize the police departments in his county from which he could draw personnel from the available pool.

Fast forward to April 16, 1984, when I received a call from Shawano County Sheriff James Knope. He wanted to address concerns he received from the county board and the district attorney about the activities of the Posse Comitatus in and around its 160-acre fenced and gated military-style compound. Complete with armed men and guard dogs, the group maintained an unlawful presence in his county.

It began three days earlier with a routine traffic stop of a pickup truck for speeding. The deputy observed a twenty-something man, suspected to be a Posse member, hauling thousands of rounds of .223-caliber ammunition. He reported the incident to Sheriff Knope inquiring what he should do. The sheriff told him to issue a traffic ticket for the speeding violation and let the man go.

On April 18, 1984, Knope contacted the FBI office in Milwaukee to gather further information on the Posse Comitatus. The agency informed him of an ongoing investigation of the group, particularly its leaders, since the shootout at Wounded Knee, South Dakota where two federal agents were killed and several others were injured.

Two weeks later, I met with Sheriff Knope to learn as much as I could about the Posse in order to present a case for the group's removal to Wisconsin Governor Tony Earl. I met with Earl in Madison on May 9 to explain the situation and request mutual aid financing to start the process. The governor gave his blessing and asked that I report any progress to him directly.

* * *

Returning to Portage County later that day I began to put a together a plan with Sheriff Knope for the removal of the Posse Comitatus. We decided to take a ride around the outside of the Posse compound, careful not to tip off our presence, and witnessed a number of prefabricated homes, a school with an American flag, and a church displaying a cross. Since only Posse members were allowed into Tigerton Dells, communications with the group were virtually non-existent.

While surveying the Posse compound with Sheriff Knope I asked him what he had in terms of violations against the group. "Zoning," he said. I contacted the district attorney and he confirmed that the Posse was in violation of building and zoning codes. He also said the group owed back taxes. I informed Sheriff Knope that such infringements were all we needed to remove them.

An in-depth investigation was necessary as to what and whom we were dealing with inside the group's "township." A trout stream flowed alongside the compound, at one point passing through a corner of the Posse's fenced property, which gave me an idea. I would have deputies pretend they were trout fishing and gather information about the group's activities.

On May 14, two of my deputies who loved to fly fish for brook trout entered the stream at a road near the compound and fished their way close to the fence. As they did, they were challenged by a Posse member wearing camouflage and armed with an automatic rifle. He asked the men why they were there without permission since the property had a posted warning that trespassers would face severe consequences. "We're fishermen," replied the deputies, "we have every right to be here." They explained that they were fishing in a navigable trout stream and that they entered the water from the bridge on County Road 00.

The armed man looked at the deputies with a nefarious smirk on his face. "There's a rifle range in here and you're real close to it," he said. "There's a good chance you might get hit by a stray bullet. If you have any respect for your lives, you'll stay away from this compound."

The deputies continued their surveillance of Tigerton Dells for four days, thankfully without incident. They then submitted reports to me on May 18. Among their observations were a military-style rifle range and what appeared to be two cement bunkers with portholes that Posse members could shoot from without being seen. There were at least three well-trained German shepherds walking around the compound acting as guard dogs, and a large sign at the entrance of the compound that read, "Jim Wickstrom for Governor."

A Diplomatic Approach

On May 21, I traveled to Madison to meet with Governor Earl and bring him up to speed in preparation for possible mutual aid. The governor asked me if I had tried negotiating the Posse off the compound. He voiced great concern over the potential for bloodshed due to the clear and present danger the group's members posed and how deeply they believed that their existence was virtuous. Earl begged me to try to negotiate them off the property without the use of force. I assured him that negotiation was my foremost intent. He acknowledged that even if such efforts failed I would still have his unconditional support.

At Governor Earl's request, I began pondering the most effective way to convince the Posse Comitatus members to vacate their Tigerton Dells property. The following day I phoned Barbara Wickstrom, the wife of Posse leader Jim Wickstrom who at the time was imprisoned for tax evasion, to try to arrange a face-to-face meeting with several Posse organizers. "You'll have to call Jim," she said. "You'll need his authorization."

A few months earlier Jim Wickstrom had been transferred from Shawano County to Milwaukee County Jail because Posse members driving in a dozen or so cars would spend each night circling the Shawano County Jail in a show of solidarity. Upon his arrival to Milwaukee, Wickstrom, a blatantly racist individual, was placed in a jail cell with six black men.

I called the jail and asked the guard to hand Wickstrom the telephone so I could explain my intent. But the Posse leader refused any correspondence. The next day Wickstrom changed his mind and actually called *me*. "Why the change of heart?" I asked.

"I can't take these dirty assholes anymore!" he replied.

"What's the matter, Jim?"

"How would you feel if you were woken up at three o'clock in the morning because there was a big fuckin' nigger pissing in your face?"

Knowing Jim's racist beliefs, I couldn't help but chuckle. I explained that I wanted to discuss the matter of the Posse Comitatus vacating its property.

"No chance, Sheriff," he replied. "We've warned you before. There are hundreds of armed men inside that compound. Is it worth risking your life?"

"Your group is going to move," I told him, "with or without bloodshed."

After a long moment of discomforted silence, Wickstrom authorized a meeting between his members and me the following evening.

In a torrential downpour, I drove to the Posse Comitatus compound at about 9:15 P.M. on May 29. I had previously informed Sheriff Knope that I planned to enter the compound alone. "Don't even think about it," he said. "You have no idea what you're getting yourself into." Knope then arranged to have three squad cars waiting outside the compound gate with four armed deputies in each car. We set the time limit at forty-five minutes. If I didn't exit the compound in that interval, they would come in to get me.

I locked my gun in my squad car and entered the compound unarmed. When I walked into Jim Wickstrom's house, a cold, uneasy feeling took over. The meeting took place in the living room with two men sitting on the couch and a man standing off to my left. Don Minniecheske, the military leader of the group, walked in and placed a tape recorder on the coffee table. He then reached into his back pocket, pulled out a .45 caliber Colt, and slammed it down next to the recorder. Minniecheske asked the purpose of my presence. I told him that his group would have to leave the compound because it was in violation of town ordinances and building codes. "What if we don't leave?" he asked. "What do you think you're going to do?"

"Force may be used if you don't leave," I answered, although the use of force was the last thing I wanted.

"Listen, Sheriff!" Minniecheske yelled. "You'll walk knee deep in blood if you try to remove us from this property!"

Barbara Wickstrom had him sit on the couch to settle him down.

A different Posse member, Delbert Larson, did his best to inflame the atmosphere of the meeting. He pointed his right index finger in my face and posed a challenge.

"Do you think you have enough firepower to come in here and remove us from our own property?" he asked. "I'd think twice if I were you, Sheriff. The people who live inside this compound aren't simple farmers they're fully trained warriors."

"No matter what it takes, I'm going to enforce the law," I declared. "If it comes down to a bloody war, I'll be the first one in. For the sake of the women and children, I would rather negotiate terms and avoid confrontation. But leave you will."

The meeting, which took about forty minutes, had ended. As I walked toward the gate to exit the compound Minniecheske followed close behind with two leashed German shepherds to make sure I departed without incident. The dogs growled menacingly with every step I took.

On June 4, I again met with the Posse Comitatus only to face the same response. The group's members assured me that they would not leave their property and there would be unspeakable violence if I or anyone else tried to force them. "We told you before," one of them said, "blood will be shed if you try to make us leave."

Apparently, peaceful negotiations were not going to be effective. It was time for action.

The Plan for Removal Begins

The next day Sheriff Knope arrived at my office to begin discussing aggressive options to remove the Posse Comitatus, well aware that it would require innumerable people and a ton of equipment.

During the planning process, we worked closely with the FBI and the U.S. Department of Justice. The FBI, in fact, described the Posse Comitatus as "one of the first organized manifestations" of a strain of extremism "espousing racial supremacy, but primarily focused on opposition to the federal government." Consequently, the bureau had documented the group as a "principle domestic terrorism concern" in the early 1980s. FBI agents had been tracking every move made by the Posse for several years and were able to provide Sheriff Knope and me with useful information.

On June 8, several agents informed me in a telephone conversation that they believed a Posse meeting was scheduled for the upcoming Sunday at Tigerton Dells. According to FBI intelligence, the purpose of the meeting was to plan a counter attack against my recent efforts to remove the group from its compound. "You wanted the Posse to leave peacefully," the agents said, "but your meetings made them well aware of your intentions. Now, it appears they're preparing for you, Sheriff. You better watch your back." It was believed that more than 200 of the group's members from outside Wisconsin would be attending the meeting. Leading up to it FBI agents flew government aircraft overhead. Using high-powered cameras, they took photographs of the license plates on many of the vehicles en route to the Tigerton Dells compound, some arriving from as far away as Louisiana, North Dakota, South Dakota, and Washington.

The FBI agents voiced concern that I might not have enough manpower to combat a possible counterattack by the Posse. "My manpower is unlimited," I told them. "As the northeast area director of mutual aid I oversee seven counties in Wisconsin. That allows me to draw on more than 400 people if necessary. If that proves insufficient, I'll simply call another director who will send an additional 400 or so from his district. I have the ability to call upon more than 4,500 deputies and 10,000 police officers from across the state of Wisconsin."

The agents were elated to hear that. The last thing they wanted was to put more of their colleagues in harm's way after the shootout at Wounded Knee.

On June 11, I convened with Governor Earl to discuss the Posse's meeting and how I tried to negotiate the group off its property, albeit unsuccessfully. I also explained that I had the full backing of the FBI, but the bureau was hesitant to react forcefully due to the agent deaths in South Dakota. Earl said a conference was about to take place at the Hill Farms offices in Madison where government officials would be discussing what to do about the Posse Comitatus. "Come with me," the governor said.

Arriving at the conference, Earl escorted me to a spacious room. Sitting at a long metal table in the center of the room were the secretary of the Division of Natural Resources, the Wisconsin State Patrol administrator, colonel of the National Guard, representatives from the state Department of Justice and Attorney General's Office, and twenty-five other heads of state. At the far end of the room stood a podium where Earl typically addressed his subordinates. The governor led me to the podium and introduced me to the crowd. "Sheriff, they're at your disposal," he said.

A roundtable discussion commenced led by the colonel in charge of the National Guard. I asked him about the availability of personnel carriers. "No problem," he said, "I can provide you with two if needed." The secretary of the DNR asked me what he could offer. I said that since we might need to expand our external surveillance a few game wardens would come in handy, as they're accustomed to working in the wild backcountry. The Wisconsin State Patrol administrator asked me what kind of manpower I would need. "None," I replied. "It's critical that we not use any outside influence. Posse members only acknowledge the Constitution, and as far as they're concerned, my deputies and I represent that Constitution. So we'll deal with the interior of the compound. However, we will need some of your people to control and redirect traffic on County Trunk 00 and State Trunk 49 prior to and during the raid. And we need to keep the area safe in case the raid turns into an all-out gunfight. We want to keep the public away from any danger."

The National Guard commander offered additional manpower as well, but I refused it. He asked me why since he could activate it at will. "All I have to do is say the word," he affirmed, "and Governor Earl will sign the declaration. You'd have as many people and as much equipment as you need."

"With all due respect," I said, "I don't want the National Guard there. That would make us a militant group facing another militant group, and that's something we don't want. Both sides will end up shooting at each other until everyone is dead. The situation is already on fire. We certainly don't need an explosion."

Everyone seated at the table nodded their heads in agreement.

The purpose of the mutual aid pact in Wisconsin was to keep the National Guard out of civil matters. Its officers had no business being in Tigerton Dells, especially since they aren't allowed to load their rifles until they see cannons, so to speak. Against a well-armed outfit like Posse Comitatus, it might prove too late. In the eyes of Posse members all government agents and their agencies—DOJ, FBI, and CIA, among others—were criminal with no jurisdictional power under the Constitution. The National Guard risked being shot on sight.

The following day I met with Sheriff Knope to put the finishing touches on a master plan to raid the Posse Comitatus compound and permanently remove the terrorist group from its Tigerton Dells property.

During the planning phase, I contacted the sheriffs from the seven northeast Wisconsin counties under my mutual aid authority. I informed each one as to how many deputies would be needed to accomplish our mission and the cost to be reimbursed from the mutual aid fund paid for by the state. I stressed the importance of maintaining the mission's secrecy and that the 120 contributing deputies would receive their assignments on the day of the raid. State troopers and local police officers were to place traffic barricades on the county roads one mile from the compound's entrance. All told, more than 150 sheriffs, deputies, state troopers, and police officers would be involved in the operation.

Since we were acting mostly on building and zoning violations, we had to be careful to protect personal property. Two home moving companies were contracted to elevate and relocate trailer homes to a storage area. Four furniture hauling trucks were on hand to load and store home furnishings. A local construction company offered bulldozers to complete the job by collapsing septic systems and filling basements with dirt.

Groceries had to be removed from the homes and protected from spoilage so a trucking company offered two refrigerated units to store and chill any frozen foods.

The local power utility was prepared to cut off all electricity inside the compound and the phone company was to sever communications to and from the Tigerton Dells property so Posse members couldn't summon reinforcements.

Local traffic would be rerouted so that the county road where the operation was to take place would be open only to law enforcement.

As a precaution, two animal control officers would be armed and ready with tranquilizer guns to sedate the large German shepherds inside the compound if needed.

The plan was set.

At 2 A.M. on June 20, 1984, law enforcement personnel met Sheriff Knope and me at the local high school in Wittenberg about ten miles from Tigerton Dells. Gathered in the auditorium for a final meeting before executing the raid we created seven special response teams (SRTs) with six deputies each who wore heavy armor for body protection. Each team was allocated a central

or northeast Wisconsin sheriff accompanied by one deputy from Shawano County to serve eviction notices to the Posse households. Standing outside would be five deputies assigned to guard the gate at the compound's entrance.

It was now 4:30 A.M. To attract as little attention as possible we used school buses to transport the deputies and workers from the phone and power companies to their assigned posts in and around the compound. By 5 A.M., everything was in place. The lock and chains on the entrance gate were removed with cable cutters and all SRTs were in. We hoped for the best, but feared the worst.

The first SRT approached the home of Delbert Larson, which was just inside the gate. When Larson came out to the screened-in porch to identify who was there, Deputy Ron Ryskoski, a 6-foot-2, 260-pound man, reached through the screen, grabbed the longtime Posse member by the shirt, and pulled him out with one hand. As this occurred, the German shepherds inside the compound began to bark and growl. So Ron went into Larson's kitchen and opened his refrigerator in search of food finding two T-bone steaks on a plate and an economy-sized package of jumbo frankfurters. The deputy began throwing the food to the dogs who promptly devoured it, becoming his best friends. Tranquilizer guns wouldn't be necessary as the German shepherds followed Ron and the other deputies around the compound like lost puppies in search of more tasty treats.

As the SRTs approached each home, whoever answered the door was served with a court ordered eviction notice. The deputies were instructed to evict all occupants and escort them to the front gate on foot. In thirty minutes, more than two dozen Posse members were removed from their respective trailers. At the gate, a final screening was performed to ensure that none of the members were escaped felons. (Two were incarcerated on outstanding warrants.) The rest of the Posse members were released just before sunrise and forbidden to reenter the Tigerton Dells compound. The officers working the roads provided protection for the individuals as they scattered in different directions down the long, winding country routes that passed through the area.

Shortly after, a deputy with a tape recorder logged every piece of food removed from the kitchen of each home. The food was then loaded into dry vans or refrigerated trucks to avoid spoilage so its owners could later reclaim it. Next came the furniture movers who documented all furnishings, dishware, and clothing. Since most of the family units inside the compound were modular, I had chainsaw workers from the two moving companies part their rooftops at the seams. Each half was then jacked up, placed on a rack, and pulled off the foundation. The township owned twenty acres of land across the road where the modular homes were wrapped and stored. As this occurred, Caterpillar D8 and D9 bulldozers pushed the block foundations into the basements and filled them with dirt. The earthmovers also dug up the septic tanks, filled them with sand, and buried them. A fence company then removed the chain link barrier surrounding the compound and a landscaping company finished the job by fine grading the property and dispersing grass seed.

Several weeks later after some summer sun and seasonal rain, the former menacing, military-style compound of the Posse Comitatus looked like a golf course.

Mission Accomplished

By 6:00 P.M., the mission to remove the Posse Comitatus was complete without incident. All told, more than 100 illegal weapons including AK-47s and AR-15s were confiscated in the raid, not to mention thousands of rounds of ammunition.

Before we left the scene, I had a deputy take a group picture in front of the sign that read "Jim Wickstrom for Governor." I posed with one of the Posse's German shepherds standing in front of me wearing my badge on his collar. The canine was thereafter proclaimed "Deputy Dog."

Later that evening I phoned Governor Earl to inform him that the mission to remove the Posse Comitatus, known informally as "Operation Clean Sweep," was a success without a single shot fired. Expecting firepower from the terrorist group, the governor was elated that we were able to remove its members without bloodshed or loss of life.

The following day I prepared a detailed ten-page report of the entire operation for Governor Earl and overnighted it to his office. On June 25, he called me asking if I could create and perform a training curriculum for the other mutual aid districts in Wisconsin. About a week later, I held my first training in Waukesha followed by second and third trainings in Madison and Green Bay respectively.

Afterward, Governor Earl wrote me a letter of commendation thanking me for helping direct the removal of a feared domestic terrorist group—a humbling accolade.

The FBI currently lists the Posse Comitatus as an active "gang" in Iowa. Assessment documentation from multiple bureau field offices also indicates that small levels of Posse activity still exist in several factions of the group across the United States.

10
MISCELLANEOUS MEMORIES

Take care of all your memories...
for you cannot relive them.

—Bob Dylan

It's a Packers Life

Wisconsin is famous for many things, among them: beer, cheese, bratwurst, and Harley-Davidson motorcycles. The state is also famous for something else: The best fans in the NFL. In a book that takes place in Wisconsin, I would be remiss not to mention the state's support of the Green Bay Packers.

In "America's Dairyland," it's all about the Packers. Being a cheesehead in Wisconsin isn't a stereotype, it's a way of life. According to research performed by Nielsen Scarborough in August 2014, the Packers, who have thirteen championships to their credit, maintain the best fans in the NFL. The research reflected three years of television ratings, merchandise sales, hometown crowd influence, and social media reach.

Green Bay, often referred to as a drinking town with a football problem, is the NFL's smallest market with a population of about 105,000, a figure surpassed by Packers fans on both Facebook (4.4 million) and Twitter (701,000). Green Bay is also the smallest professional sports market in North America.

During the 2013 NFL season the Rev. Quinn Mann of the Catholic Diocese of Green Bay brought Sunday mass to the fans that were tailgating in the Lambeau Stadium parking lot. An experience to behold, the reverend's smoldering incense blended perfectly with the aroma of grilled kielbasa and homemade chili hovering above the parties whose members set down their beer to pray.

There is no sports experience like a Packers game at Lambeau Field, home of football's "frozen tundra." In attendance on any given Sunday are 82,000+ fans who love the Packers more than life itself. The deafening sound of their voices can be heard for a country mile. The waiting list for Packers season tickets, currently at more than 110,000, exceeds the population of Green Bay itself.

If your diet consists of bratwurst smothered in mustard and sauerkraut, you know all the words to the Beer Barrel Polka, and you know who Ralph Bruno is, you can consider yourself a fan of the Green Bay Packers—America's most historical NFL franchise!

Starr Struck

On March 18, 1986, I flew to Boulder, Colorado to attend the National Institute of Corrections since I planned to build a new jail in Portage County. During the flight, I had the privilege of meeting former Green Bay Packers quarterback, head coach, and NFL Hall of Famer Bart Starr. On his way to a business meeting, he was sitting in first class doing work out of a leather briefcase. Walking the aisle on the plane when I noticed him, I struck up a conversation with one of my favorite sports heroes. The discourse was short and to the point.

"Bart Starr, how are you? I asked.

"I'm fine, thank you," he replied. "Who may I ask are you?"

"My name is Dan Hintz, sheriff of Portage County in central Wisconsin."

"Thanks for your service," Starr said.

I expressed gratitude for all he did to help establish the Packers' winning legacy.

"Thank you for the compliments," he said. He then offered me a handshake and returned to his work.

Walking back to my seat I thought, *Wow, I just spoke to and shook the hand of one of the greatest men ever to play the game of football!* Then it occurred to me: How stupid not to ask for an autograph!

Bill and Hillary Clinton

September 1991

Shirley and I had the honor of meeting Hillary Rodham Clinton at the University of Wisconsin—Stevens Point where she had stopped to campaign on behalf of her husband Bill in anticipation of the 1992 presidential election. We talked at length about life, law enforcement, and politics, and my wife was thrilled to receive Hillary's autograph on the cover of a program pamphlet.

The following day we met Bill Clinton at the American Legion in Stevens Point. An articulate speaker, Bill retained a personal charisma and passion for politics much like John F. Kennedy in that his followers listened intently to what he had to say, hanging on his every word. When Bill spoke with you, he made you feel like the most important person in the room—an assessment I've heard many people make about him. He looked you in the eye as if he was confiding in you, confident in what he said without appearing egotistic. I felt as if he understood me as I understood him.

Meeting the Clintons was an experience that Shirley and I will never forget.

A Place to Call Home

Growing up in small town America provided me with the perfect launching pad to mold my life into whatever I wanted it to be. As a young man, I couldn't wait to leave Shantytown, but looking back, I realize it was the best place to spend my childhood. As I approach the big 7-0, I know I will never forget the tiny hamlet that meant so much to my life.

I moved to Florida some thirteen years after my law enforcement days. But my love for Shantytown, the Village of Plover, Portage County, and the state of Wisconsin never wavered. The experiences I had there—good and bad—the laughter and the tears, all contributed to the adult I became and the family I tried my best to raise.

The most important lesson a small town can teach you is the notion of a place where you belong. Life can offer a plethora of changes and opportunities, but there is something special about knowing you always have somewhere to call home.

Should've Known Better

July 2000

My wife and I flew back to Wisconsin for the funeral of one of my longtime friends who lived in Plover. When we arrived at the home of my sister and brother-in-law where we were staying, we noticed that we had forgotten to pack a few items for the trip. So I hopped in the car and headed out on Highway 54 to a local convenience store to do some shopping. Out of the blue, I spotted a Wisconsin state trooper on the shoulder of the road. In my rearview mirror, I could see he had turned around and was pursuing me. As I proceeded to slow down, he pulled me over. "Do you know how fast you were going?" he asked.

"No sir, I don't," I replied.

"You were doing 65 in a 50 zone."

"I'm truly sorry, sir," I said. "After spending nineteen years in law enforcement I guess I should've known better."

The trooper asked where I was headed. "I'm visiting from Florida to attend a friend's funeral in Plover."

"Do you want the next funeral to be your own?" he asked.

"No sir, I don't."

"Then slow down!" he yelled.

"Yes, sir, I sure will."

"I'm gonna let you go with a warning this time," he said with a stern look on his face. "Don't let me catch you doing it again."

"Thank you, sir. I appreciate your kindness."

After all the citizens I had pulled over for speeding through the years, you would think that I'd be smart enough not to speed myself. Never so embarrassed, I drove away in silence, fortunate only to receive a warning.

11

A Family Decision: Leaving the Job I Loved

Don't simply retire from something;
have something to retire to.
—Harry Emerson Fosdick

It's true that law enforcement officers exist to protect and serve, but the truth is that they can't protect everyone. They have not only a duty to protect the public, but also the loving families they come home to at the end of each shift.

By late 1986, my family felt that I was too involved in law enforcement. I was president of the Wisconsin Sheriffs' and Deputy Sheriffs' Association and the Badger State Sheriffs' Association. I was also northeast area director of mutual aid and a member of the Polish Legion of American Veterans. Occupied nearly every weeknight and weekend, it got to the point where in order for me to see my son Kevin, my youngest child, I would have to take him with me to some of my meetings. Being sheriff of Portage County was no longer a job it was a way of life. And because of it, my family found itself on the back burner.

One night at the dinner table in December, I said to my family, "We're going to hold an election when we finish eating. I want you to think about whether I should pursue another term as sheriff."

It was a 3-2 vote.

My son Kevin and I wanted to see at least one more term. But the women, my wife and two daughters, wanted me to walk away and enter the private sector. The Village of Plover could use a good sports shop, they argued, especially one that sold bait and tackle. In the Hintz household, as in America, democracy wins. For the better part of two decades, my family supported me in my quest to protect and serve, never questioning my decisions. Now it was time to do things their way. I began making plans to leave office and walk away from the job I loved.

What my family explained made sense. Through the years there were so many things that we wanted to do or had planned to do but couldn't because of my job responsibilities or a meeting that required my presence. After all, law enforcement isn't a 9-5 job. Too many times, as I headed home at the end of my shift, my wife would have dinner on the table and I would receive a call to report with deputies to the scene of an accident or a crime. Even though my wife understood the importance of a sheriff to serve and protect she often questioned why my deputies couldn't take care of such incidents. The answer was simple: I was the person who had to answer for them. Reporters weren't going to call the deputies in the morning to ask about what happened at the scene, they were going to call the sheriff, and I needed to be prepared to offer answers.

Last Day as Sheriff

On January 1, 1987, I walked away from law enforcement forever. Unable to sleep the night before, I woke up at dawn thinking about how I would say goodbye to my colleagues.

An emotional day from the moment I walked into the sheriff's department, I spent the morning packing up personal items I kept in the office including my nameplate and some family photos on my desk. My desktop was void of any documents and trays. Barren walls now surrounded me. It felt eerily empty. Walking out the door my eyes welled with tears as I glanced over my shoulder to take one final look at the office where I spent the most important part of my life.

I turned in my .357 caliber revolver and sheriff's badge and cleaned out my glove compartment of personal items as well as my .20-gauge pistol grip. I spoke with Tom Wanta, my replacement as sheriff, concerning any final questions he might have. I told him he was going to be fine and that I had all the confidence in the world in him. I walked down the hall and wished everyone well. Stan Potocki, the department captain, then gave me a ride home. When I got out of the car, it hit me like a ton of bricks: I no longer had a department to oversee. Colleagues would no longer approach me with questions or problems. Moreover, I was no longer employed! For a fleeting moment, I had second thoughts about my decision to walk away. I remembered the hard work I put into my election campaigns: the first where I defeated the "unbeatable" incumbent sheriff, the second in which I was challenged by big corporate money yet won handily, and the third when a detective from my own department ran against me. But the forth term where I ran unopposed was the one that bothered me the most. I was fully secure in my position as sheriff, yet I gave it up. At the same time, however, I thought, *What a load off my back! No more headaches! No more worries! I get to spend time with my family!*

Reflecting on my time in law enforcement, I realized there was much more to the job than a uniform and a badge, especially when not everyone respects an officer's authority. It was stressful and testing at times, but through it all, I'm still here. And I believed that happened because of support from my family and my faith in God and Jesus Christ.

In my heart and soul, I believed that I could have retired from my job as sheriff of Portage County. But the unconditional love I shared with my family was just as important to me as getting criminals off the streets and solving crimes that brought closure to victims and their families. I was ready to embrace the next chapter of my life.

Epilogue:
Life after Law
Enforcement

The most important thing is this:
to sacrifice what you are now for what
you can become tomorrow.
—Shannon L. Alder

More than sixty years ago I knew I wanted a career in law enforcement—a decision I have never regretted. It started with a desire to make a difference by preventing or stopping crime, arresting those who violated the law, and pursuing justice against those that harmed others. To stand up for those in greatest need represents a critical vocation, but for me it wasn't just a job, it was a way of life. It was who I was. The reason I chose the profession—with its substandard pay, long hours, endless stress, and potential for danger—was a call to duty, compelled by a desire to assist the public. If I had the chance, I would do it again in a heartbeat.

When I first started in law enforcement, I thought the profession was about "protecting and serving," making a difference in the world. On the surface it undoubtedly was. But it was also an opportunity to see myself through the people of my community, a chance to address my deeply held beliefs about life and death, and the constitution of my country.

Despite facing many dangers on the job, I never feared death. Although I have in no way looked at myself as anything special, I felt that being killed while protecting the public I was obliged to serve would be the ultimate way to die. Even so, after nineteen years in law enforcement my health and life remained intact, so I wanted to enjoy whatever time I had left in this crazy world.

* * *

My nineteen years in law enforcement allowed me to see brutality at its worst and humanity at its best. It was the good things about humanity that allowed me to believe my occupational responsibilities were worth doing. Yet thinking back on some of the most profound incidents of crime I confronted—murders, shootings, assaults, and drug trafficking to name a few—it makes me wonder why such crime occurs. I don't think I will ever find an answer.

* * *

Drug enforcement was one of my greatest pursuits as sheriff. Several drug busts in Portage County during my eight-year tenure helped limit drug trafficking in central Wisconsin. They were accomplished under the combined efforts of the sheriff's department, the Wisconsin Department of Justice, the Wisconsin Drug Enforcement Agency, and other police and sheriffs in Wisconsin.

But the achievement I am most proud of is the removal of the Posse Comitatus. Its systematic investigation and planning involved a number of sheriffs and police agencies as opposed to the more traditional handling by state and federal agencies. When I was elected as the northeast area director of mutual aid, I had no idea I would be helping to direct a situation of this magnitude.

That being said, it's easy to revel in the good. Still, I always question if there were some things I could have done better. Even though I strove to be honorable and ethical, I made plenty of mistakes. In the end, however, I did my best to do right by the public I was elected to serve.

* * *

After spending two years in the private sector, I decided to run for the position of Portage County court clerk in 1989. But the assistant clerk crushed me, officially putting an end to any further public service aspirations.

In March 1987, I opened Plover Bait and Sporting Goods at the intersection of Highways 51 and 54 in Plover. The shop started small but soon expanded into a large retail sports store that carried guns, ammunition, loading supplies, and featured indoor archery and shooting ranges.

After receiving a solid financial offer for the store in the summer of 1990, I sold out and went to work as a dispatcher for J.P. Mach, a local trucking company. For two years, I worked twelve-hour shifts, six days a week, plus two hours on Sunday mornings before church.

Fed up with my long hours Shirley handed me a newspaper clipping in September 1992 for a car salesman position that was open in Stevens Point. At first, I thought she was joking but she insisted that I would be good at it. The dealership, Cooper Motors, interviewed me and lo and behold, I was offered employment. Although I had no sales experience, I took to the job like water, setting sales records after my first twelve months. In the summer of 1995, Courtesy Motors, located just across town, heard about my success, and offered me an opportunity to manage one of its dealerships, Courtesy Mazda and Nissan. After nearly five years on the job, I retired to Florida in March 2000.

Calling it retirement, however, wouldn't exactly be accurate. I wanted to enjoy my later years but I didn't want to fall off the grid. I'm still a faithful husband and devoted father and I keep busy with local business endeavors. I also love to hunt and fish. As my friends and family will tell you, I don't like to be idle.

Through it all, it is my hope that I am remembered more as a good sheriff than a good politician. But I learned along the way that you have to be both; it was all about gaining the trust of the public.

I am grateful for the opportunity to have been Portage County's sheriff for four terms, and overall, the nineteen years I served in law enforcement in my home state of Wisconsin—all in pursuit of justice!

A Few Thoughts on the
State of Law Enforcement in America

When you have police officers who abuse citizens
you erode public confidence in law enforcement.
That makes the job of good police officers unsafe.
—Mary Frances Berry

It was my intention to write this book based on facts, not opinions. But after spending nineteen years working in law enforcement I would be negligent not to include a few thoughts on the current state of the police vocation in America.

It wasn't too long ago that the most powerful weapon law enforcement possessed was its capability to communicate with people. But contemporary technology has caused some officers to become lazy in the sense that less legwork is needed in accomplishing their job. Personal contact with the public doesn't seem to be there anymore. The notion "for the people" appears to have gone by the wayside in favor of an "us vs. them" mentality.

Police and the public need each other. It's a symbiotic relationship. When officers don't get out of their cars and walk among the public they become out of touch. Law enforcement officers can't get to know people by use of the internet. A computer can't break up fights, settle disputes, bandage wounds, or perform CPR. Officers need to get back to walking the beat and riding bicycle patrol near America's schools. They need to know the current generation of children for they are the key to the future of our nation's law enforcement.

I used to love it when members of the public took the time to tell officers to "be careful out there" or simply say "thank you" for the job they were doing. Today, unfortunately, the public and media too often look for a story where an officer makes an error, either while working, or in his or her personal life. It's understandable that officers of the law are held to a higher standard. They should be. They're hired to protect the public. But some of these errors are inevitable and they can place officers squarely, and unfairly, in the public eye—on radio, television, or at the mercy of a journalist's pad and pen. And all the details of the story might not be available. It's a part of the job that most citizens will not understand. It seems that too many officers are more worried about avoiding trouble than being preemptive and averting crime. It's my hope that one day soon that will change and we can return to the days when officers can focus solely on "protecting and serving"—just as they're hired to do.

Much of the public doesn't understand what it means to have to make a life or death decision in the blink of any eye only to have it scrutinized and, in some cases, criticized for years. I fear that in the years to come law enforcement officers will continue to lose their lives because they will hesitate in making a life or death decision for fear of public retribution. They will pause and think for a split second that in reality they do not have, in the process, leaving behind loving families.

Various news accounts have chronicled how local police departments across America have obtained from the military a disconcerting array of surplus equipment. Why, exactly, does a small-town department need a mine-resistant vehicle or a grenade launcher? It's tough to justify.

But perhaps more dangerous than the equipment is the entrenched disrespect that some of today's law enforcement officials seem to have for the public they are hired to serve and protect. It's becoming a complex problem, and the militarization of today's police is a symptom of that problem. Officers that don't follow the law—those that wrongly inflict damage upon ordinary citizens with basic police gear—are that much more dangerous with military equipment in their possession. The current federal programs that outfit police departments with military gear are wasting government funds and propagating mistrust between law enforcement and the communities they're hired to protect.

This is why many Americans see law enforcement officers as indolent, unscrupulous, doughnut-eating buffoons who spend their days on egocentric, gun-toting power trips. Worse, it's perplexing to hear cops dismiss such criticisms with phrases like "come walk in our shoes before you say anything." The difficulties of your job are no excuse for operating like a paramilitary force.

Billions of dollars of excess military equipment and questionable funding to buy even more has made its way to local police departments over the past two and a half decades. Originally, Congress approved such funding as a way to help departments outgunned by drug gangs. After the terrorist attacks of Sept. 11, 2001, the flow increased as lawmakers spent more money to help police prevent further terrorism. But such programs have now gone too far. All local law enforcement officials have to do is simply ask to buy ambush-protected vehicles along with battle uniforms similar to military fatigues and they're approved by the government to do so with Department of Homeland Security funds. When you factor in a contemporary command structure that allows such alarming behavior to intensify, it's a disaster waiting to happen. Not to mention that providing such equipment to a police force comes at a steep cost. Officers dressed in military fatigues will be viewed as the enemy in most any community. These days, it seems that police seldom, if ever, think about the reaction that such an unnecessary deployment of force is bound to induce.

It would be reckless to infer that every police force in America is striving to become militarized. Not every force seeks to do so. But they don't have to. Those that already have are enough to send the wrong message to our nation's public.

It's not my intention to sound like an old man pining for the good old days, but I remember when most cops had revolvers and weren't so quick to discharge hundreds of bullets into an American citizen in a mindless panic. Police supervisors need to make certain their officers aren't acting as overbearing control freaks that refuse to tolerate even the slightest indication of disrespect, and to ensure that those officers aren't wasting taxpayer money by working against the public instead of for it. All citizens are innocent until proven guilty. I think that sometimes many of today's police forces tend to forget that.

Every week, it seems, brings a news story about a police choking, beating, or the false arrest of civilians. It's the advent of a dangerous problem: the belief that the increasing use of power against a civilian is justified no matter the violation. Too many of today's law enforcement officers don't seem to understand that in numerous instances, such aggression is the cause of the ensuing escalation and subsequently they wind up shouldering more responsibility during the inevitable adverse outcome.

Good law enforcement officers feel a sense of duty and commitment to community service. They are driven by a strong and sincere motivation to help better the lives of other people, and make a positive difference in the world, be it large or small. They must be able to adapt quickly to new and changing situations while displaying sound judgment and reasoning under extreme pressure. A good officer possesses integrity, confidence, compassion, reliability, and patience. Success in the occupation of law enforcement will be difficult, if not impossible, without these traits.

Law enforcement isn't a game. Officers must be mentally and physically prepared each day for whatever the job throws at them. There must also be a devotion to training and practice. After all, there's no easy way to be a good officer. The more that law enforcement officers sweat in training, the less likely they are to bleed on the street.

Some officers might appear indifferent to the tragedy at hand. To the public they might seem apathetic and unemotional as if they don't care or that the tragedy doesn't affect them. None of this is true. Officers genuinely want to help society. That's why they became officers. They will never become wealthy in their line of work and they know that some people will hate them simply because of their occupation. Yet they decide to become officers anyway because they feel they have a chance to make a difference in their communities, their nation, and in the world.

The individuals entrusted to "serve and protect" their communities from criminal activity are human just like everyone else. That means they are capable of making bad choices or behaving unethically just as much as anyone else. But since police uphold an obligation to enforce the law it's reasonable to believe that they cannot concurrently violate the law and enforce the law with their actions. What would happen if everyday citizens took the law into their own hands and used excessive force in doing so? Some of those citizens would be called vigilantes. Most would be called criminals. There is no excuse for making exceptions when the individuals committing crimes happen to wear badges. Such crimes should be equally condemned for the sake of those that perform their occupation honorably.

It's true that there are good officers who honor the badge and bad officers who don't. But those that fulfill their duty as officers far outnumber those that don't. And those that don't should be held accountable for abusing their power. As in most professions, good officers will tell you that they have no tolerance for rogue colleagues.

The dark side of law enforcement always looms. The occupation is filled with honest officers who lose their way. The challenge is to resist the temptations and go about the job in an ethical manner.

Acknowledgments

I would like to acknowledge the late Bill Bablitch, former Wisconsin Supreme Court justice, state senator, and Portage County district attorney. The support I received from Bill during my first three sheriff campaigns proved critical in my election and reelection bids.

A sincere thank you goes out to Dave Helbach, former Wisconsin assembly member and state senator, for his assistance during my elections. Dave and I ran for our respective offices concurrently and campaigned together. Without his help, I'm not sure if I would have been successful in my bid for sheriff.

A thank you also goes out to Gary Wescott for his support and trust in me on the Sunday night forum at WSPT Radio in Stevens Point. Gary taught me good public communications, which I have never forgotten.

Even after more than thirty years, I must to extend a heartfelt thank you to former Wisconsin Governor Tony Earl for his unwavering support during the removal of the Posse Comitatus.

Good friends are hard to find and impossible to forget.
This book is dedicated to the memories of…

William Bablitch

I was fortunate to meet Bill at the onset of my law enforcement career. We became good friends during his run as district attorney from 1969-1972. In late 1972, Bill ran successfully for state senator. An ambitious politician, he served in that capacity until 1983 during which he helped write child abuse legislation and modernized the antiquated Wisconsin Rape Law. He was elected to the Wisconsin Supreme Court in 1983 where he served until his retirement in 2003. Bill passed away in February 2011 at the age of sixty-nine.

Robert Sankey

A close and dear friend, "Bob" was instrumental in my campaigns through all four terms that I served as sheriff of Portage County. He and I used to cut firewood together that we used to heat our homes; hard work, but we enjoyed every minute of it. Bob passed away from cancer at the age of sixty-two.

Mike Giese

Another of my friends who worked hard on my campaigns, Mike and I fished and hunted often and through the years became very close. The man would do anything in the world for me and me for him.

When I started the Plover Police Department, he was there to help in any way he could including service as my animal control officer. When I decided to run for sheriff, Mike worked tirelessly on my campaign every day after work posting signs and handing out thousands of pieces of literature. Mike passed away in December 1987 at the age of forty-two.

Sheriff Facts

- As of January 2012, there were 3,080 sheriffs in the United States.
- Currently, there are only four U.S. states where sheriffs do not serve four-year terms: Massachusetts (six-year term), Arizona and New Hampshire (two-year terms), and New Jersey, the only state with a three-year term.
- There are three states in America that do not have a Department or Office of Sheriff: Alaska, which has no county governments; Connecticut, where a state marshal system replaced the position of sheriff in 2000; and Hawaii, where deputies serve in the sheriff's division of the state's Department of Public Safety.
- The position of sheriff is not mentioned in the U.S. Constitution.

(Data furnished by the National Sheriff's Association, http://www.sheriffs.org/content/faq)

Law Enforcement Facts

- There are more than 900,000 sworn law enforcement officers now serving in the United States, which is the highest figure ever. About 12 percent of those are female.
- A total of 1,501 law enforcement officers died in the line of duty during the past 10 years, an average of one death every 58 hours or 150 per year. There were 100 law enforcement officers killed in 2013.
- On average over the last decade, there have been 58,261 assaults against law enforcement each year, resulting in 15,658 injuries.
- The 1920s were the deadliest decade in law enforcement history. A total of 2,390 officers died, or an average of almost 239 each year. The deadliest year in law enforcement history was 1930, when 297 officers were killed. That figure dropped in the 1990s to an average of 162 per year.
- The deadliest day in law enforcement history was September 11, 2001, when 72 officers were killed while responding to the terrorist attacks on America.
- New York City has lost more officers in the line of duty than any other department, with 697 deaths. Texas has lost 1,675 officers, more than any other state. The state with the fewest deaths is Vermont with 22.
- Since the first recorded police death in 1791, there have been more than 20,000 law enforcement officers killed in the line of duty.
- Presently, there are 20,267 names engraved on the walls of the National Law Enforcement Officers Memorial.
- There are 1,081 federal officers listed on the Memorial, as well as 622 correctional officers and 32 military law enforcement officers.
- There are 275 female officers listed on the Memorial. Four female officers were killed in 2013.
- During the past ten years, more incidents that resulted in felonious fatalities occurred on Thursday than any other day of the week. The fewest number of felonious incidents occurred on Tuesday.

(Data furnished by the National Law Enforcement Officers Memorial Fund, current as of May 2014, http://www.nleomf.org/facts/enforcement/)

People often approach me and ask, "Since you used to work in law enforcement, can you offer some advice on how to avoid getting a traffic ticket?" Here are some **<u>common sense</u>** tips on how to avoid a ticket and, potentially, arrest if pulled over for a traffic violation:

- Be respectful.
- Produce any requested documents without argument.
- Don't smile as though the situation is funny.
- Don't tell the officer his equipment must be malfunctioning.
- Don't tell the officer *your* equipment must be malfunctioning because you could be cited for an equipment violation, which, in some cases, might cost more than a speeding ticket.
- Don't use the excuse, "the accelerator must have stuck." It's the oldest one in the book.
- Don't say, "I'm late, I have to go now."
- Don't say, "I know people in high places."
- Don't say that you hold a high society position.
- Don't ask officers for their badge numbers.
- Resist the urge to ask, "Don't you have better things to do?" or "Don't you have murderers, rapists, and terrorists to chase?"
- Don't argue that the officer must have the wrong person.
- Don't say you are experiencing pain and need to reach the hospital, because you should have called 911. Worse, the officer might escort you to the hospital and issue the citation there.
- Financial bribes won't get you anywhere, so don't offer money to the local police department or to the officer personally.
- Let the officer know that you understand it is his duty to enforce the law.
- Remember that you are at the mercy of the officer who pulled you over. Show the officer some appreciation.
- Be humble and admit your mistake. Politely ask the officer to write you a warning, and promise to never again repeat your mistake.
- Above all, be honest, apologetic, and sincere. Address the officer as just that—"officer." Respect the fact that law enforcement officers are human beings. They have emotions and feelings even though they might not always show it.

(It might sound obvious, but remember to always obey local speed limits, use turn signals, and wear your seatbelt.)

Dan Hintz served in law enforcement from December 1967 to January 1987 as a deputy, a police chief, and the sheriff of Portage County, Wisconsin. He was also president of the Badger State Sheriffs' Association and the Wisconsin Sheriffs' and Deputy Sheriffs' Association.

Born and raised on a small farm in central Wisconsin, Hintz served two years in the U.S. Army including a stint as a communications specialist in South Korea.

Hintz and his wife Shirley live in Florida.

John Spiller is an author, media entrepreneur, and consumer advocate. He is the author of *The Ampersand Diaries: AT&T and the Life Lessons Learned from the Trenches of an American Icon* and founder and president of media and publishing company The Working Hour Media Group.

Spiller lives in Florida where he retains an unhealthy obsession with law enforcement.

Dan Hintz

inpursuitofjusticebook@gmail.com
facebook.com/inpursuitofjusticebook

John Spiller

theworkinghourmediagroup@gmail.com
facebook.com/johnspiller3
twitter.com/spillerbooks (@SpillerBooks)